Meditations of Anselam

Letters from
an
Elder Teacher

David C. Jones

DETSELIG
ENTERPRISES LTD

Meditations of Anselam
© 2005 David C. Jones

Library and Archives Canada Cataloguing in Publication

Jones, David C

Meditations of Anselam: letters from an elder teacher/David C. Jones
Includes bibliographical references.
ISBN 1-55059-289-0

1. Self-realization--Religious aspects. 2. Spiritual life. 3. Conduct of
life. I. Title

BL624.2.J66 2005   204   C2005-903090-9

 Detselig Enterprises Ltd.
210, 1220 Kensington Road NW
Calgary, Alberta T2N 3P5

Phone: (403) 283-0900
Fax: (403) 283-6947
Email: temeron@telusplanet.net
www.temerondetselig.com

We acknowledge the support of the Government of Canada through
the Book Publishing Industry Development Program (BPIDP) for our
publishing program.

We also acknowledge the support of the Alberta Foundation for the
Arts for our publishing program.

SAN 113-0234
ISBN 1-55059-289-0

Printed in Canada   *Cover Design by Jon Paine*

Introduction

Anselam is really a composite character embedded in my life-time of experience and reading. He is like a higher self with memories and insights born of joy and sorrow, of error and delight, with a mind turned now toward the light. Whatever he may have thought at the time, he was always happiest in the light. Like all teachers, he needs to forgive himself for what he did if it met not his ideals, then to march on making fewer and fewer mistakes, offering more and more uplift and insight, joy and enthusiasm, delighting in every contribution, his own and his students' – ever expanding himself, his sense of wonder, his interests, his love for students, his respect for himself, his trust in them, and in himself.

These letters are the meditations of Anselam. By turns, they vibrate as simple stories, parables, metaphors, dramas, and as a gentle counsel to action in the life journeys of Alma and Arn, two beginning teachers.

David C. Jones

Drink in the ozone, bathe in the sunshine, and out in the silent night under the stars say to yourself again and yet again, "I am part of all that my eyes behold," and the feeling will surely come to you that you are no mere interloper between earth and sky, but that you are a necessary particle of the whole.[1]

Elbert Hubbard

Both Should be Fulfilled

Dear Alma and Arn,

May I congratulate you on your wedding and thank you for including me. Now you are both teaching in the same city, Alma, in a grade three class, and Arn, in a high school, a fulfillment of the first of your dreams. Next, you will become the teachers you want to be.

You both asked how to be all you can be, so as you begin this magnificent career let me say – never see your interests as apart from anyone else's.

It is in the best interests of a teacher and a student that both will succeed, that both will shine. Yet how many teachers and students see their purposes that way? How many teachers who survey their own classes the first day of school or college, and on subsequent days when things seem strained, when clashes jar the peace, when personal problems loom – not only wish the best for their charges, but do the best for them? And how many students on that first day, and on subsequent hard days, have the best interests of their *teachers* at heart, want *them* to excel, and are willing to do everything possible to facilitate that excellence? How many students actively seek the best for their instructors? And where is this ideal taught? In a world of egos and separateness there is much learning involved in seeing your interests as the same as another's, yet in a fundamental sense what else should a teacher and a student desire but the flourishing of each other? *Both* should be fulfilled.

These things you might say in the first days to reveal a powerful and beautiful *intent*.

Blessings, *Anselam*

The Song of Your Students

Dear Alma and Arn,

Alma, you wonder what you "are trying to do," and Arn, you say the opening weeks have been "one confusion after another."

May I suggest a focus?

Jack Kornfield tells a story in *A Path with Heart* about a sense of belonging, a sense of place within a community of souls.

"There is a tribe in east Africa in which the art of true intimacy is fostered even before birth. In this tribe, the birth date of a child is not counted from the day of its physical birth nor even [from] the day of conception, as in other village cultures. For this tribe, the birth date comes the first time the child is a thought in its mother's mind. Aware of her intention to conceive a child with a particular father, the mother then goes off to sit alone under a tree. There she . . . listens until she can hear the song of the child that she hopes to conceive. Once she has heard it, she returns to her village and teaches it to the father so that they can sing it together as they make love, inviting the child to join them. After the child is conceived, she sings it to the baby in her womb. Then she teaches it to the old women and midwives of the village, so that throughout the labor and the miraculous moment of birth itself, the child is greeted with its song. After the birth, all the villagers learn the song of their new member and sing it to the child when it falls or hurts itself. It is sung in times of triumph, or in rituals and initiations. This song becomes a part of the marriage ceremony when the child is grown, and at the end of life, his or her loved ones will gather around the deathbed and sing this song for the last time."[2]

May your classes embrace this sense of belonging, of social togetherness, of the forming of supportive and respectful relationships. May they cultivate the beauty and the value of each single soul. "Realize your uniqueness in the entire universe," J. Donald Walters once said. "No one will ever have your song to sing: through all eternity it is yours alone. Your primary task in life is to learn that song, and to sing it perfectly."[3]

What is the song each of your students would sing?

Blessings,

Anselam

Being Right or Being Kind

Dear Alma,

So you have set up your rules, your routines, your expectations in your first week, and you ask under what conditions would you disgard your deadlines, regulations, requirements? Is a student's sickness enough? A student's bereavement? A misfortune? A disability?

I once had a rule that in order to pass senior high school English, everyone in the course had to do a major presentation in front of the class. One girl, who was in the early stages of pregnancy (she was unmarried), refused to comply, and therefore failed the course. Now, I was aware of the rumor of her pregnancy, and she was definitely not her normal self and slept through most classes, which seemed to confirm the suspicion. But in my immaturity, I applied the same rules to her as to everyone else, and justified them on the unstable grounds that she did not "look" pregnant, she was not "showing" and could thus make the presentation to class, appearing "normal."

Of course, I estimated poorly her tormented and utterly downcast state of mind, her deep embarrassment. The joint effect of the unexpected child and her failure in English seemed to delay her progress in life. At a reunion I attended twenty years later, she was actually physically shorter than she had been in school.

Now, had kindness had its way, I would have been less concerned about being "right" in applying the rule. In fact, I would not have considered being right as being important at all. I would have released her from the rule and given her a test of equivalent rigor that did not require her to "display" herself while completing the course. I would have been immensely more sympathetic and caring.

Many years later, after I had become a university professor, a similar situation arose. I had a rule that in order to pass my course, each student had to complete the main assignment and the final exam. Now, one of my students was also a soldier, and on exam day he was at camp, hundreds of miles off. He arranged to sit the exam on return, and I gave it to the secretaries to administer. When he arrived, he went directly to my office, and because the term was over, I was not there. Rather than ask the secretaries who were on the same floor, where I was, he left immediately for the local military base. Later that day, I read his note on my door, and I tried to call him at the base. His whereabouts seemed to be the nation's main military secret, and no one in camp would connect me to him, despite my good intentions.

In the end, I had a choice – I could be "right" and fail him for not completing the two parts of the course, or I could give him the benefit of the doubt and award him a course mark equivalent to the one he had achieved on his major assignment. This time, kindness prevailed, and I gave him the mark. I never saw him again, but I never regretted my decision.

In the case of the young woman, whom I was fond of, a sense of peace eluded me for thirty years, despite my apology to her at that reunion, and my prayers asking for forgiveness. In the case of the soldier, peace was mine the moment I was generous.

Blessings,

Anselam

Energy Loss and Gain

Dear Alma,

You have taught now for two months, you feel drained, and you wonder if an extended holiday might rejuvenate you.

What induced the energy loss? Most think that work itself causes exhaustion, but a much greater source is the ego investment in your thinking and action. Doing things as a teacher for the benefit of your ego is always tiring – for example, helping a student so that you might impress a parent, or preparing a remedial reading program so that your principal will notice, or working overtime so that bystanders will applaud, or volunteering for the teachers' association so that your resume will swell. Acting primarily to be valued, or planning primarily to be honored, or living primarily for appearances – all will dispirit you. Why? Because they suggest that something outside yourself gives you worth, and you fear you may not find it: that approval, that confirmation. So you are ever dressing for your public, not for yourself.

There can be another source of energy loss, related to your own enthusiasm, strangely enough. Everyone who knows you has felt your exuberance. It is your gift to them. And they are grateful for it, even the worst of the curmudgeons. Why? Because your enthusiasm is the clearest and most exhilarating sign that you are *alive*. On seeing you, the dispirited and the depressed instinctively know *that* is how to live. Many are dying the slowest and most agonizing death from ennui; they have been terminally ill for decades, and their illness is boredom. They see that you are not bored. They want your energy, and they draw it from you, and the drainage tires you. You can prevent it by creating, with your mind, a shield around yourself.

In the meantime, just be yourself, and the attractiveness of your personality and way of being will affect certain people for the better. You are a natural healer, with a fragrance of your own, but that fragrance can heal only those who are attracted to it.

I myself am attracted to it. Have you ever noticed how playfulness engages you, how games delight you, how the simplest things underfoot captivate you? Have you ever watched how you linger with fascination at the things around you, the trees in the sunlight, the grass waving in the breeze, a water beetle, a crocus, a buffalo pod? Have you ever acknowledged your friendliness, or the fact that you really do love the trees? All these honest interests are what give you your vitality.

But remember, even your enthusiasm, the cream of aliveness, will sour if you insist that it be someone else's ideal. Share your aliveness, and laud the enthusiasms of others, but do not *demand* that your interests be theirs.

I think the great lesson you will teach by example is something like this – it is good to be enthusiastic about a thing or two, but better if enthusiasm is part of what you *are* and how you greet many things. Expand your curiosity, interests and fascinations, because enthusiasm is an unfailing measure of your own self-chosen capacity for delight. As Helen MacInnes said, "Nothing is interesting if you're not interested."[4]

Love,

Anselam

Remembering

Dear Alma,

May I say one more thing about enthusiasm?

The quality of being interested is, of course, related to memory. How valuable is your memory, and what do you want to remember?

There is a story from the Hindu tradition about a conversation between Arjuna and his master, Krishna. At a time when people lived longer than they do now, Arjuna was eighty-five years old, or middle-aged, and he had long noticed with awe and admiration the incredible mind of his master.

"Lord," said Arjuna, "how is it that you can remember all the past lives, and I cannot?" Now, he was referring to the Hindu belief of having lived before, but also, to the million things that happen in a single lifetime.

Krishna answered, "Ten years ago, on the third day of the month, what were you doing?"

"I do not know," said Arjuna.

"Well you were alive then," Krishna said.

"Yes, I was alive."

"Look back, Arjuna, sixty years to the day you were married, do you remember that?"

"Oh yes," replied Arjuna, "I remember that."

"Then look further back, Arjuna, to the day you met your guru and were taught the martial arts. Do you remember?"

"Yes, I remember."

Then Krishna noted, "It is obvious that men remember that in which they are interested, that in which they are sufficiently intense to cause them to remember the incident. But that in which they are not intensely interested, they do not bother remembering....*Now I remember everything, Arjuna, because I am interested in everything.*"[5]

What you remember about anything is related to your ability to teach it, to give it life, and what you remember about anyone else is related to the thoughtfulness you can show, the respect.

Your memory is related to your ability to love. It is extremely difficult to tell yourself, by force of will alone, "I will love this person or that." You need to know something about the person, something about his motives, fears, delights, sentiments, and the more you know, that is, the more you remember, the more you can care.

Love,

Anselam

Human Negative Need

Dear Alma,

Have you ever recognized that when you focus on what you *do* instead of what you *are*, you often feel weak? If you constantly get satisfaction from doing, rather than being, you may be rewarded while you are doing, but what happens after, when you are no longer doing what you did? You feel at a loss, wondering how to revive that sense of uplift, engagement, accomplishment; so you try to do more to feel right, but you have taught yourself that you only feel right when you are constantly working, without rest or respite.

That is only part of the problem. The real difficulty lies in *why* you are doing what you are doing. Have you asked yourself that? Are you doing it because you think someone else will approve: a parent, a teacher, an administrator? Are you doing it because the system will smile? Are you doing it, basically, for someone else? I am not speaking here of service to those in need; I am speaking of doing something so that others will think you are a fine soul, a caring teacher, a responsible administrator.

This is *human negative need*, and it absolutely pervades our lives. You say you are giving gifts to your students – books, crayons and the like. Why? So they will like you? Confirm you? Is it a bribe so they will be amenable, so they will tell their parents how generous you are, what a wonderful teacher you are? If it is, it is human negative need.

You have just done your first in-service workshop on children's literature. Are you fixated on the reaction of the teachers in the in-service, and do you feel if they don't approve, you have some- how failed? If so, that is human negative need.

You see, the need is negative because it depends on the reaction and whim of others, and if you invest your whole personality in it, you make yourself utterly dependent on the reaction. Then you are very weak.

You need to validate yourself from within, to know that what you are doing is valuable and worthwhile, or you would not be doing it. You need to move into positive human need, into doing things because you want to do them, because they make you more of who and what you are, because they give you joy and fulfillment. And when you are more of who and what you are, when you expand yourself, when you feel enthusiasm and delight, then you can serve others with verve. Tending exclusively to the needs of others will leave you tired and undone. Value yourself first, then you can serve others knowing that that same value is in them too.

Blessings,

Anselam

Giving with the Result in Mind

Dear Arn,

Your students are "ingrates," you claim, and you are furious with their "universal lack of appreciation" for what teachers do for them.

Every teacher is a gift-bringer, whose task is to discover what to give, and then to accept what the learners receive of the gift. In turn, what learners can accept, blended with their own offerings, is what they can bring to their relationships.

Think of this: your giving is weakened by any form of regret over the act, because regret is a wish that you had never given at all. The more intense this wish, the tinier the gift. And regret can take different forms – one being that whatever was given is lost forever; others, that the receiver will not appreciate the gift, will not use it "properly," will not return it somehow, or was not worthy of it in the first place. "Gifts should be handed not thrown," says a Danish proverb.[6]

"It is not the function of . . . teachers to evaluate the outcome of their gifts," says *A Course in Miracles*."It is merely their function to give them. Once they have done that, they have also given the outcome, for that is part of the gift. No one can give if he is concerned with the result of giving. That is a limitation on the giving itself, and neither the giver nor the receiver would have the gift. . . . Who gives a gift and then remains with it, to be sure it is used as the giver deems appropriate? Such is not giving, but imprisoning."[7]

You know, "You can have a car, son, if you go to medical school." "I'll give you marks, student, if you tow the line. I'll respect you, if you honor my magnificence." "I'll love you daughter, if you do these things. But the moment you don't do them, mommy won't like you!"

Many people, teachers included, withdraw their gifts the moment they don't receive lavish thanks, eternal gratitude, instant response. But who are we as teachers to judge the outcome of our gifts of hours, dedication, counsel, energy, encouragement, expertise and enthusiasm? Who are we to judge the outcome, or to time it? *Or to time it?* What will you do if a student doesn't respond to your advice in an hour, a week, a month, a year? Withdraw the gift in anger or irritation? I've seen a case where it may have taken twenty years for a student to fully appreciate a teacher, twenty years to really love a teacher.

Blessings,

Anselam

Gordon's Gift

Dear Arn,

What was the case, you ask. Fifteen years ago, I was at a reunion of the 1971 high school graduating class I had taught. Sometime in the ensuing twenty years, one particular student was touched by a teacher he had perhaps only begun to appreciate in 1971. This student was part of the "do your own thing" resistance to authority of that time. I don't know when he was reached, I don't know when the teacher's gifts became clear to him, I don't know when he accepted them. I can only say that the teacher – Gordon Fleet was his name – had touched me too. He was my close friend, he was older, and he became my ideal of gentleness in a male. Maybe this same trait attracted the student, who was now a police sergeant, whose cup overflowed with violence and whose experience with serenity and gentleness had perhaps been all too brief. My friend Gordon died at age 95, a few years ago. Completely unassuming, he was constitutionally incapable of insisting that his gifts be used "rightly."

Cheers,

Anselam

Ellen's Gift

Dear Alma,

You are right. Rules, conventions, and outside conditions can limit our giving, if we allow them to. Often you need to honor these conventions, and sometimes not. Take, for example, your Anglo North American fears about touching a student.

My daughter has reached the age where she may decide what to do with her life. Now, *I* know she would be a great teacher, probably a primary teacher, like you, but she may not know this. Though we both know she has to experience things herself. So, I asked if she would like to volunteer with Ellen, a Calgary teacher who had been a university associate, helping us with our teacher-training programs. Ellen is a marvelous teacher, so positive and compassionate, you can see the glow. We met her at the school where I introduced her to my daughter. Just before this grade one class began, a little girl came in, looking pale and piqued. She was crying, so Ellen picked her up, sat her on her lap, with the little girl's head resting on Ellen's shoulder. Whoever had brought the girl warned she might be sick again, and I learned that the day before, the girl had vomited all over the room and all over Ellen. I watched this little person swallowing fast, a sign for me as a youngster that I would soon be throwing up. The threat had no effect on Ellen at all. She held that child as if it were her own, and it did not matter if another suit might need cleaning. So unconditional was the love, that I know my daughter Abbie had seen one of God's saints.

Love,

Anselam

Opening to the Truth

Dear Alma,

You have quoted one of my favorite parts from *Conversations with God*. I too was so attracted to the same statement some years ago, that I repeated it to myself and others on impulse.

It is one of those majestic outpourings fed by an eternal spring. If spirituality were not meant to be self-chosen, I would insist that everyone memorize it. For the footsore and thirsting, it refreshes, reminds.

"Relationships are constantly challenging; constantly calling you to create, express and experience higher and higher aspects of yourself, grander and grander visions of yourself, ever more magnificent *versions* of yourself. Nowhere can you do this more immediately, impactfully and immaculately than in relationships. In fact, without relationships *you cannot do it at all*.

"Relationships are sacred because they provide life's grandest opportunity, indeed its only opportunity to create ... the experience of your highest conception of self."[8]

"Did God really say this?" you ask.

I don't know. It is what I would like *my* God to say.

But if there is a God, one of the greatest inquiries you can undertake concerns what He or She is, what His or Her will is, what the world might be if you were like your Creator. If there is a God, how would He express His own highest ideals? Even if there isn't, how would *you* express yours?

Some might consider these ideals to be truth, so what is truth to you? Where do you stand, and what do you stand for? These questions you need ask, whether or not you think God spoke these words to Neale Walsch, the writer of *Conversations*.

Does it matter where the truth comes from? "Be open to the truth, no matter who is speaking it," J. Donald Walters once wrote. "If you smell smoke, and a parrot squawks, 'The house is on fire!', is that the moment to reassure others, 'Oh, but the parrot doesn't understand what it is saying?'"[9]

With Affection,

Anselam

The Real You

Dear Alma and Arn,

In deciding where you will stand, you begin to define yourself.

A Course in Miracles says, "Any situation must be to you a chance to teach others what you are, and what they are to you. No more than that, but also never less."[10]

You are a consciousness with innate worth and prodigious creative power. Project something other than this, project who you are not, and you will see misery. Project weakness and you will see a frightening world; project impotence, and you will be unable to ward off danger; project powerlessness and you will be afraid; project worthlessness, and you will receive your just reward: frustration and failure.

How you see yourself determines *what* you see. *What* you see tells you *how* you see yourself, because it is always in relationship to what you see. What you believe about yourself determines what you see. See yourself as you really are, and you will see the world as it really is. See yourself as whole, healthy, loving, powerful and invulnerable, and what can you see in the world to frighten you?

Being whole, what demands will you make? Those who are whole make none.

Blessings,

Anselam

P.S.

Would these thoughts help?

"You are a spark of an eternal flame. You can hide the spark, but you can never destroy it."[11]

Paramahansa Yogananda

"However broken down the spirit's shrine, the spirit is there all the same."[12]

Nigerian proverb

Hearing the Inner Voice

Dear Alma,

You are teaching in a Catholic school, and this is your opportunity to witness to your own philosophy. A student has asked, "What is the Inner Voice?"

You and I need to answer this question (and any other question) according to the nature of the person who asks.

So to you, who have always been intensely interested in finding God, I will answer one way; to Arn who is uneasy with discussions of God, I would answer another way, if he should ask.

This line from *The URANTIA Book* resonates with you, Alma:

"Never forget there is only one adventure which is more satisfying and thrilling than the attempt to discover the will of God, and that is the supreme experience of honestly trying to do that divine will."[13]

You have repeatedly felt the truth in this statement, so to you I say, that the Inner Voice is the Holy Spirit. To Arn, I might say, it is his sense of the truth, his true self, his higher self, or his higher consciousness.

A passage in *A Course in Miracles* captures the nature of this higher consciousness: "The Voice of the Holy Spirit does not command because it is incapable of arrogance. It does not demand, because It does not seek control. It does not overcome because It does not attack. It merely reminds."[14]

Learn what this Spirit is, and you will know more about the God you love; learn what the Spirit is, and you will understand the meaning of respect. Your school regularly upholds respect as one of its mottos, does it not? You have posters in your room and in the halls emblazoned with the word "RESPECT."

One facet of respect is the absence of arrogance, or conceit, because arrogance is another word for *disrespect*, and conceit means forgetfulness of others. Another facet of respect is the absence of the impulse to deny another the right to think and to choose, even if the choices are wrong. (Now, in a school, children need to be protected against certain harmful, even potentially fatal decisions, but they still need to *choose*, and to choose wisely. A vast range of choices should be allowed, choices that may lead them temporarily astray, but not too far astray – choices with consequences they can understand, bear and change.)

A third powerful facet of respect is the absence of any disposition whatever to attack another person, to assault, insult or overrun. In *The URANTIA Book*, Christ refuses to take advantage of the human mind by overwhelming it with such a record of human achievement and wonder-working that it *must* believe, that *any fool would believe*, despite his honest reservations. Jesus respected his family too much to dazzle them with his resume, to bowl them over with a full, glorious account of the larger part of his life not recorded in the gospels. Each soul must be allowed an honest reservation, if he should entertain one, and each one must be allowed to come to an honest conviction.

Such a show of irresistible glory and magnificence would be tantamount to an attack, a presumptuous and undue attempt to compel belief. It was not what he had *done*, but what he had *taught* that was most important. The teachings themselves were aromatic and inviting, and they were never meant to compel, but rather to attract. When one chose to be attracted, one was transformed by the beauty of the teaching. Likewise, you as a teacher can so deluge your students with evidence, stun them with irrefutable argument, stagger them with your splendor that they cannot think for themselves. But if you press them to that point, you will not have respected them.

Nor will you respect them if you use your great musical and athletic abilities, your degree in musicology, or your championship in basketball, as a reason for them to believe your message, or as a demonstration of the truth you are speaking.

Love,

Anselam

Probing Your Beliefs

Dear Arn,

Faith, one of your outspoken colleagues says, is a concern of the religious, and he is an agnostic who feels very uncomfortable when the word "faith" comes up. In the same breath he adds, after a single term, that he has no faith in your administration and little in your colleagues. It is "so ironic," he claims, that he has moved from his previous school where he substituted for six months, and where the administration was "deceitful and uncaring" and the staff was "plodding and mediocre" to find after only four months, similar sins in your new school.

First, may I say that "ironic" is not the right word; "consistent" would be better. He consistently finds these "failings" because he *expects* them. And he does have faith despite his denial, but it is a faith in human shoddiness and incompetency. Faith is born as a belief, and when it proves itself, as it soon does, it becomes ingrained, and then it becomes a personal dogma that one proclaims to anyone who will listen, and some who will not. Sadly, some of the students are listening. And one of your youngest colleagues is listening. These are this man's converts – and he says he has no interest in religion! And in his social studies classes, he condemns to the fires of Hell all the world's attempts at conversion.

Just be aware of what is happening here. Do not criticize the beliefs or this man, and do not join his thought system.

Mistrust is a faith too, though it might better be called the faith of the faithless. A positive faith is very important to you now – call it a *belief* if the word "faith" offends.

The function of a belief system, of faith, is to lead you, however circuitously, to the truth, and when you know the truth and experience it, you will reach an inner certainty. When you are there, you are in your own heaven, where beliefs are meaning-less, except as a way to get there. In this bliss, doubt does not exist, or it would not be bliss.

Every teacher is a beliefs shepherd.

Whenever a student or colleague believes he is unable, unpro-ductive, unhelpful, unappreciated, unworthy, or unloved, the teacher gently and confidently offers a more attractive alternative. She nurtures a belief system, however timid and trembling at first, that sincerely and joyously embraces capabili-ty, accomplishment, caring, comforting, respecting, valuing and affection.

A student may never know his own value until you respect him. He may never realize his thoughtfulness until you notice it. He may never acknowledge his creativity until you show it to him.

You can probe your own beliefs too. Write them down. Discover the ones most basic to your interpretation of the world, your core beliefs. I say "discover" because many of your own beliefs are hidden, categorized as characteristics of the world which you take for granted, when they are, in reality, your *interpreta-tions*, your beliefs *about* the world.

Look closely to see those beliefs that are affirming, and those which are not. Whatever the belief, it will already have proven itself to you.

Blessings,

Anselam

The Power of Belief

Dear Arn,

You are too inclined to dismiss the notion of beliefs as wispy and insubstantial. Books have been written about the biology of belief, and you might consult Herbert Benson's work. (See for example, *Timeless Healing: The Power and Biology of Belief*, 1996).

All beliefs have effects, but to appeal to your sense of the dramatic, let me speak of negative beliefs. Australian Aboriginal witch doctors have been known to "point a bone," to cast a spell on a victim. The spell can so disturb the spirit of the victim that disease and death can result. In 1925, Dr. Herbert Basedow witnessed a case:

"The man who discovers he is being boned is, indeed, a pitiable sight. He stands aghast, with his eyes staring at the treacherous pointer, and with his hands lifted as though to ward off the lethal medium, which he imagines is pouring into his body. His cheeks blanch and his eyes become glassy, and the expression on his face becomes horribly distorted. . . . He attempts to shriek but usually the sound chokes in his throat, and all that one might see is a froth at his mouth. His body begins to tremble and the muscles twist involuntarily. He sways backwards and falls to the ground, and after a short time appears to be in a swoon; but soon after he writhes as if in mortal agony, and covering his face with his hands, begins to moan. . . . His death is only a matter of comparatively short time."[15]

This is a macabre effect of a belief, but all beliefs, beneficial ones too, whether true or false, have effects. And there are any number of studies demonstrating the effects. In 1950, Dr. Stewart Wolf studied women who experienced persistent nausea and vomiting while they were pregnant. These women were given a drug that they were told would cure them. In reality, they took syrup of ipecac, a substance that *causes* vomiting. Astonishingly, the nausea and vomiting completely ceased.[16] Belief alone was enough to induce the cure.

You might say, "Interesting, but what's it got to do with me? And what's it got to do with teaching?" A lot, because you and all other teachers have beliefs and expectations, and these all have effects you may not be aware of.

Blessings,

Anselam

Eeyore Teachers

Dear Arn,

Good for you! You have made a list of your beliefs and are surprised at what you have found. Yes, you have reasserted your belief that you will succeed, however long it takes. This is a basic confidence in yourself, though you will notice it is seeded with an expectation that it *takes* a long time to succeed. Keep the first part of the thought and release the second. Do not predetermine or prejudge how long it might take. That is an artificial limitation, a governor on your creativity. If you want to do anything at all, assume an early arrival.

You have identified a cynical strain in your thinking that you say you were only partly aware of. Others around you have seen it too, often sooner than you did, because invisible beliefs in a person are usually visible to friends.

You ask a fundamental question – how can you stop thinking the way you do; how can you stop thinking cynically? Before we go into this, be sure you have mapped all your beliefs, because we will need this map in answering your question.

May I also suggest that you are not as cynical as you say. There is too much natural excitement, too much in-built delight for you to ever be a terminal cynic. So, what I offer may help as much in understanding these terminal types, as in adjusting your own perspective.

In order to stop thinking cynically we must change the ground level beliefs that are the terrain on which we tread. Our beliefs and expectations are the self-made landscape we traverse. We have trudged over it and waded through it so often that we think it is reality, that it was there before we were – yet it first appeared with our thoughts and was created by them. If we have become a terminal cynic, we are that landscape with its immobilizing mishmash of deadfalls, its treacherous bogs, its stupefying humidity – shadeless, breezeless, unrelieved. In this sense, we, the observers, are the observed; we are what we see.

Now, "unrelieved," in your case, is inappropriate. Your relief is your cynical sense of humor that diminishes misery by laughing at it. You really do think that Dame Edna's statement is funny: "I was born with a priceless gift – the ability to laugh at the misfortunes of others." Or Voltaire's: "I was never ruined but twice: once when I lost a law suit and once when I won one." Or the anonymous: "A monastery is a home for unwed fathers." Or George Bernhard Shaw's: "The English are not a very spiritual people, so they invented cricket to give them some idea of eternity." Or, Frederick Raphael's: "Awards are like hemorrhoids; sooner or later every asshole gets one."[17]

Your cynical sense of humor does protect you in a certain way. Perhaps you have heard Jean-Paul Sartre's comment about a certain woman: "She believed in nothing; only her skepticism kept her from being an atheist."[18] A tendency to negate everything, including atheism, can be a benefit. You do know how difficult it is to believe *not* in God and *not* in atheism, simultaneously. So reason alone will show you the moral bankruptcy of cynicism. This is worth emphasizing, and I am delighted you are doing just that.

You can carry this thought further.

"Both the cynic and the idealist believe in disarmament," said Robert Quillen. "The difference between them is that the idealist believes it will work." "More than any other time in history, mankind faces a crossroads," added Hubert Allen. "One path leads to despair and utter hopelessness. The other to total extinction. Let us pray we have the wisdom to choose correctly."[19] For a cynic wishing to escape cynicism, these are cynical comments worth memorizing.

You speak of an older colleague caught in the self-defeating, self-immolating, repetitive loop of deadly cynicism. Have you noticed that there is no easy way through his landscape? There is no high road, low road, or middle road; no path, no trail, no milestone; no survey post, no guideline, no guide; nothing he can count on except a tangle of trouble. A strange masterpiece it is, this stumbling-block world he has created. You see, the mind can do anything, and he gave it the task of creating chaos in which it could actually appear to be able to do nothing, and lo, he has succeeded. He has taken something of infinite power and asked it to be powerless, and because it has infinite power, it has done so. What he has created should actually encourage you, because clearly you can materialize a world of *complete unreality*, a world totally out of synch and inconsistent with the natural conditions of your being. And you can create another world too, in synch with what you really are.

With affection,

Anselam

P.S.

You say the Eeyore teachers, the black cloud critics, the doom-sayers, appear to enjoy their suffering, and you ask how anyone could enjoy suffering. Perverse as it seems, it is the joy of a grim viewpoint being confirmed by a grim observation. So it is the joy of being right in conveying bad news. What the Eeyore teacher is saying is, "See how rotten things are! See what I have been stating for so long! See how correct I am!" It is rather like gloating over losing your arm, after you told everyone that the machinery was more dangerous than they thought.

This is another reason why you should not worry quite so much about being "right" all the time.

Deeper Yet

Dear Arn,

Your friend says cynicism is really realism, and most cynics would agree, but does he know the deadly *effects* of cynicism?

Most cynics are down with the "flu of the carping critic," and few crave their company. One day a Hindu, a Jew and a Cynic chanced upon a farmhouse in a downpour, near dark. The farmer had beds for two in his house, but the third would have to sleep in the barn. So the Hindu volunteered for the hayloft.

Minutes later, there was a knock on the door – it was the Hindu who was uncomfortable disturbing the sacred cows in the barn. So the Jew went out, but he too returned, unable to sleep with pigs, whom his religion deemed unclean. Then the Cynic tramped to the barn.

Seconds later, there was a commotion and another knock on the door. It was the cows and pigs.

Cynicism is the enemy of all great teaching.

It is a form of attack – an attack on others, as well as oneself.

Cynicism is the belief in the futility of human thought and endeavor. As a plan of action, cynicism is meaningless, because to a cynic nothing works. As a reflection of what he thinks of others, it is demeaning, because to a cynic everyone is a fool. As a judgment on himself, it is equally degrading, because everyone who believes in the futility of his own thought and endeavor must also believe in his own *impotence*.

Every thought that your life's dream will not come true, that the worst side will triumph, that a task must be redone a dozen times before it is right, that what you buy will be flawed, that your life is never right, that you are bound and can never be free, that people are fools, that the universe is chaotic, that bad things always happen to you, that life is thankless – is one mark, then two, then a dozen, confirming a continuing cynicism.

The cynical engage in a form of self-sabotage. They have become very adept at seeing obstacles, and they give those obstacles great power; in fact, more power than they themselves have. In this sense alone, terminal cynics are giving. They have a remarkable ability to find difficulties where others do not see them. Because they have removed the power from within themselves to outside themselves, they are very fearful. They see many things to fear, and they see those fearful things winning in the end. Theirs is a very frightening world causing them to be constantly on guard, constantly arming. In the end, they fear even their own ability to forecast all the ways the world must thwart them. The convolutions and complexities of existence are so overwhelming, so malignant, so inexorable, so inescapable.

As an instructor, the calloused cynic leaves little hope for her students. Some she sees as hapless incompetents, others as cheats and connivers, still more as middling and mediocre, so far beyond their depth in a pathetic school system and a malicious world. Her tragic viewpoint, the cynical teacher constantly teaches, though she may never realize how pervasive a life perception is. What you think the world is, you will teach. If you think nothing is achievable, you will teach futility. If you think there are horrible forces constantly threatening, you will teach fear. If you deem beauty of character to be always fouled in some way, you will teach suspicion. If you mistrust your pupils, you will tell them, one way or another.

What inspiration can such a teacher be? What can he accomplish? What faith has he? What trust? What hope? What sense of personal value?

If he doesn't respect his pupils, how could he ever encourage self-esteem in them? If he won't trust them, how could he ever engender self-confidence in them? If he doesn't love them, how could he ever instill a natural friendliness? Keeping things from them, how could he ever cultivate openness in them? Constantly condemning them, how could he ever comfort them? Counting them as incompetent, how could he ever hearten them? Seeing them as incapable of victory, how could he ever rally them?

You see, all these thoughts are inside the cynic: the hopelessness, the futility, the anger, the aggression, the sense of personal worthlessness. The lashing out comes from an interior condition; that is why we call it lashing out. The rottenness and the corruption are his own views, his own interpretation. In a very important sense, they represent the way he processes his world. They are not out there; they are part of him.

Here is a notice from the Foothills Hospital. At the top of the page, the patient's name is given. Then the letter says, "Please be advised that your Oprectomy operation is scheduled for 8 a.m., May 1, 2008. The purpose of this delicate operation is to sever the cord that connects your retinas to your rectum. Hopefully, this will get rid of your shitty outlook on life."[20]

You see, the deep cynic looks at the world through fecal lenses. What he sees is part of himself.

And the poor cynic, there he is lashed to the piling of a barnacle-infested wharf as a fetid tide of decay and pollution rolls in relentlessly and laps about his throat and nostrils before it covers him. The last reality he senses in that split second between the inhaling of this stinking scum and the loss of consciousness, is that the stench and the rot are now inside him as well – *where they all began.*

Blessings,

Anselam

Being Made Divine

Dear Arn,

Having reached an all-time low, we now need some rehabilitation.

Has a cynic any value? Only a cynic would say no. He has the same value and the same sanctity that all have, and he can possess highly refined skills.

No one can capture the idiocy of inherently stupid practices better than a witty cynic. Cynics can laugh at misfortune, at human frailty, human ineptitude and human ignorance. And laughter can dissolve pain.

A cynic is a litmus paper that turns red in the presence of human hypocrisy – hypocrisy oft hidden by self-deception. If you be the hypocrite, the cynic simply tells you; and if you have been deceived, now you are undeceived – though you may, of course, remain a hypocrite.

One may receive a cynic's comments as a personal insult, or as an aid to self-understanding. If we take the latter view, when a cynic speaks, rather than recoil, we might *listen*, ask if he has seen something we may have missed, ask if he tells the truth about life, about the human condition, about *ourselves*.

Arthur Balfour once said, "It is unfortunate, considering enthusiasm moves the world, that so few enthusiasts can be trusted to speak the truth."[21] Do not react to the apparent negativity; do not arm – the fear in arming will consume you, immobilize you, deafen you. Listen. Ask, *when does enthusiasm lie*? In your own enthusiasms, or mine, have we ever said too much? In our own promotions, have we ever misled?

"Gratitude is merely a secret hope of further favours," said Rochefoucauld.[22] What is the nature of your gratitude . . . and mine? Does it seek to manipulate? Is it cunning? Is it a trade masquerading as a gift? Is it disingenuous, really unmeant, and therefore dishonest? These questions need asking, if we would purify our intent.

The great cynic Ambrose Bierce said that to consult was "to seek another's approval of a course already decided on."[23] Is that true, when we as administrators "consult"? If so, is our appeal not misrepresented and disrespectful? You know, I do not really want your opinion unless it is mine.

"The evolving soul," says the massive *URANTIA Book*, "is not made divine by what it does but by what it tries to do."[24] Anyone, including a cynic, who directs your attention to your motives is helpful. What did you strive to do? What did you attempt? That is the measure of human evolvement, not what you did. Do not focus overmuch on externals, on what happens, because what will you do if the outside darkens? Many things happen in life – a project may fail, a program may falter, a job may be forfeit, even a war may be lost. All these are results, or partial results, of what you did. But what did you try to do? Where was your heart?

When I think about a coach of one of my boys, I think about differences we had over coaching and about some results that seemed unsuccessful, but then I recall the noon hour my son ran into a huge tree, going full speed after a football – it could have been fatal.

And I remember the deep caring and kindness this coach showed, as he helped my son and informed my wife of the accident. And I remember this same coach calling me at 1 a.m. on the coldest January night in two years (33 below Celsius). The basketball team was returning from a tournament, and the old bus the coach was driving had broken down. I can still see him out there in the freeze, directing players into parents' cars that were arriving half an hour later. He knew what to do, and he knew who to call, and we knew something of his spirit, his steadfastness. You only have to see that once, and you know who the person is, forever.

Blessings,

Anselam

Spying

Dear Arn,

So your cynical friend mistrusts his students and has begun a system of espionage on them to discover who may be cheating on his exams.

Elbert Hubbard once said, "There is one thing worse than to be deceived by men and that is to distrust them. When you grow suspicious of a person and begin a system of espionage upon him, your punishment will be that you will find your suspicions true."[25] He meant that people find what they want to find. And mistrust is a punishment, because it is frightening and calls forth inordinate energy in worry and foreboding and the construction of defenses. Mistrust is fatal; it is faith in fear and kills by exhaustion.

How much extra time do you think you would need to be sure things are right, if you didn't trust the person doing them? Mistrust is poison to a teacher, especially when it is accompanied by statements of affirmation about pupils and their abilities.

Your friend is writing reports to your principal, detailing the malfeasance of certain students. This spying activity is dangerous to his peace of mind, and be assured, peace of mind is something you will want sooner or later. Over time, spying is very hard on the psyche because it is exceedingly judgmental and judgmental without recourse. No student response is possible to clandestine communiqués, and so the secret messages to the principal utterly disrespect the invigilated. They are a kind of trial where the accused is undefended and silent, and cannot hear the verdict and does not know he has been condemned. They are a violation of trust and resemble the cold work of a sniper. Great offence occurs in spying – the betrayal of everyone, even the students one appreciates but embroils in the problem, and that betrayal inevitably begets intense, even insupportable disharmony in the mind of the betrayer. When once the magnitude of the offense is grasped, the road to recovery can be long. "The worst about a double life," Hubbard said, "is that the relationship makes the man a liar. The universe is not planned for duplicity – all the energy we have is needed in our business, and he who starts out on the pathway of untruth finds himself treading upon brambles and nettles which close behind him and make return impossible. The further he goes the worse the jungle of poison oak and ivy, which at last circles him round in strangling embrace."[26]

Mistrust is a form of separation, and you must do everything, Arn, to *join* with your students, to become part of them and their lives. George Eliot once asked, "What loneliness is more lonely than to distrust?"[27] As a teacher, be very wary of separation. The psychologist Erich Fromm once said, "The deepest need of man is the need to overcome his separateness, to leave the prison of his aloneness."[28] *A Course in Miracles* goes further: "All sickness comes from separation. . . . Depression is an inevitable consequence of separation. So are anxiety, worry, a deep sense of helplessness, misery, suffering and intense fear of loss."[29]

When you see a young person – one of your students who is not well-regarded, who has no friends, who has been shunned and ostracized – watch carefully, be sensitive and help. Go out of your way to recognize those who are ignored by others. Your note suggests that the one your friend is watching so closely, is such a person.

Blessings,

Anselam

Some Suggestions

Dear Arn,

How to be more positive, you ask.

First, you might study some of the masters I have encountered. Perhaps you are like me and want to see a living exemplar. Undoubtedly, the central teaching of masters such as Yogananda, Maharj, the sage known as The Mother, Aurobindo, Sai Baba, and the writers of *A Course in Miracles* and *The URANTIA Book*, is that the core spirit of humanity is sacred, divine. All these masters and others manifested throughout their lives, abilities beyond the "expected" accomplishments of the common humanity. All demonstrated that the limitations we accept, they did not. All sought to expand our tiny sense of individuality. All believed that even the harshest of circumstances was incapable of upsetting the equanimity of the truly self-assured. None came with a message that what they taught could not be learned.

Second, you could cultivate graciousness, "the aroma of friendliness that emanates from a love saturated soul." It is graciousness that gives your natural goodness its power. "Goodness always compels respect," says *The URANTIA Book*, "but devoid of grace it often repels affection. Goodness is universally attractive only when it is gracious . . . effective only when it is attractive."[30]

If you want uplift, walk down the hall with a certain PE teacher in Cochrane, as I did, and the friendliness is so unmistakable, it is transforming. Then look at the track and field banners for umpteen straight years in that school. Look at the student participation. I arrived the day they began preparations for the spring meet, and Mr. O asked the PE class how many wanted to go in the 3000 meter race. That race is so taxing it can be fatal. One year, Calgary officials cancelled it altogether. At the beginning of the 1000 metre race at our school, the starter gave as his last instruction, "Don't throw up on the track!" So how did the students answer Mr. O's call in Cochrane? Half the class volunteered, and the other half paced the volunteers!

Third, "develop a sense of community with others," says the sage J. Donald Walters. "See that community as consisting of more than your little family, more than your neighborhood, more than the town or city in which you live. Expand your sense of community to include, finally, the entire world."[31] Do it a bit at a time, as the best of our school travel clubs do.

One day, Pat McMahon, a radio talk showman in Phoenix hosted Mother Teresa, and he begged her to allow him to give her something. Finally, she said, "Tomorrow morning get up at 4 a.m. and go out onto the streets of Phoenix. Find someone who lives there and believes that he is alone, and convince him that he's not."[32]

Love,

Anselam

P.S.

You might avoid the gossip that sometimes arcs through staffrooms, remembering, as Baba says, that the discussion of evil in others always tarnishes one's own mind.[33]

What to Accept from Others

Dear Arn,

You have been trying to make sense of the welter of messages you get in a day – the compliments, the rejection, the judgments, the suggestions, along with all the affection and fury, the helpful and the hateful, the predilections and the pessimism with which they are projected. To this chaos, you want to know how to react. What should you accept from others?

You might want to accept their insight on an issue, but not their obsession with it; the wisdom of their criticism but not the venom in it; their wit, but not the scorn; their self-analysis, but not the self-centredness; their depth of analysis, but not their depression over the analysis; their service to others, but not their lament over the hardships of duty. Take whatever is helpful from what they say, and leave the rest.

Blessings,

Anselam

Changing the World

Dear Alma,

You do have the potential to change the world, but it is important to know how this can happen. "Morality can never be advanced by law or by force. It is a personal matter, a free will matter," says *The URANTIA Book*, and "it is disseminated by the contagion of the contact between morally fragrant personalities and those less morally responsive, but who are also in some measure desirous of doing the Father's will."[34]

One way you advance is by being attracted to the fragrance of another, and you choose that fragrance. The way you will change the world thus, is through the beauty of your own personality and your relationships with others. Certain people will be attracted to your vibrancy, your exuberance, your kindness, your tolerance, your generosity, your joy, and the world will change as each single soul seeks, and then manifests, even one of these virtues. Then each, too, will hold out that trait as a gift for those who in some sense, even slightly, are already revealing it.

My Affection,

Anselam

A Mistake

Dear Alma,

Did I ever made a mistake as a teacher?

More than one, as you may have noted.

I once had a student in grade 12 English class, and while he was no scholar, he was a delight because he had a great sense of humor. He energized the group, gave it sparkle, life. He was an ally that a teacher sometimes needs, someone on your side who stirred things up, who could nudge another student from apathy to engagement, from thoughtlessness to awareness. He was like an actor bringing the audience into a play. He was animated, and you could not ignore his enthusiasm. He was artful, I now think, and gifted.

In those days, there were no provincial or state examinations, at least where we were. The wholesale attack on the establishment that reached a crescendo in the late 1960s, had shattered the school curriculum and the authority of state-imposed regulation and assessment, and so we, the teachers, controlled more of education and its offering than you now do. Of course, there was still an English curriculum, and there were still books to cover, including my favorite, *The Iliad*, but we had no external examinations to fear, so we did what we liked. With outstanding teachers, the results were as inspiring as any uplift of the schools in the previous century. With weaker teachers, the results were disastrous. In general, standards fell, the Beatles sometimes replaced Shakespeare, and writing and literacy skills deteriorated for most of a decade. Masses of students graduated not knowing what a sentence was, and some became teachers, who naturally could not light the lamps of students more brilliantly than their own were lit.

In the arrogance of youth, I considered myself one of the "better" teachers. After all, I still taught sentence fundamentals – dangling modifiers, misplaced modifiers, agreement faults, antecedent faults, punctuation faults and the like. But with this one student, Jim, I became one of the "worst" teachers. I cannot explain it properly to you, nor has it been easy to forgive myself.

It came time for our little final examination in English. This examination was meant to be something more than a meaningless exercise, but it was not intended to be the principal determinant of success, of passing or failing. To this point, Jim had received passing grades – C's as I recall – nowhere near brilliant, but also nowhere near collapse. Well, he wrote my final examination, and he handed in almost a complete blank. I was shocked and offended that nothing of my "brilliance" had rubbed off – not a concept, a thought, nor a single word. *A disgrace*, I said to myself, *an incomprehensible and complete zero, nothing learned*, and I wrote that on the report card for his parents, and failed him.

Now, of course, he could not graduate. I remember his mother coming around and saying how it upset him, and I remember my self-righteous reply. Justice had spoken, and my mind was set in concrete.

Jim took the class again the next year, but he seemed wounded and dispirited. Bit by bit, the gravity of what I had done seeped into my consciousness. For a year, the lad had been an ally – one I greatly appreciated – and when I failed him in the end, it was like betrayal. The final examination did not warrant the weight I attached to it, but then no one can bear the weight of another's pride.

Avoid at every turn, Alma, taking offense at what a student might do.

With Sad Remembrance,

Anselam

A Teacher's Fears

Dear Arn,

You asked if I was ever afraid as a teacher. Most assuredly, I was.

We all know the effects of fear. "Fear is the worst enemy," said the great guide Silver Birch. "Fear corrodes. Fear impedes the channel through which help can come. Fear disturbs the physical, mental and spiritual atmosphere around you. Fear is the enemy of reason. Fear prevents that calmness of outlook and resolution of mind that are your greatest allies in your life."[35]

Have you ever noticed how people's minds are filled with phobias? There is claustrophobia, agoraphobia, arachnophobia, Iraqnophobia, technophobia, aquaphobia, pyrophobia, necrophobia, ballistophobia, Russophobia, Anglophobia, Francophobia, and perhaps there is even omniphobia – fear of everything. No wonder Rama said, "The brave alone enjoy the world."[36]

Teachers, too, have fears. Some teachers are like cooks – afraid to share their recipes; a few are like jailers – afraid of the inmates; some are like psychiatrists – afraid of what they might find in themselves; and a few are like cynics – afraid of impotence, everyone else's, and, ultimately, their own.

Many teachers are afraid to change, afraid to be open, afraid to solicit criticism, afraid to loosen up, afraid even that students might discover the questions they ask on exams. In many universities, it is difficult to find old exams on sociology or psychology, and often in other subjects as well. Imagine being afraid to show students the kinds of questions you ask!

I've looked at myself and at my own fears. At one time, when lecturing was virtually the exclusive method of instruction at the university (in some quarters it still is), I would create a presentation as close to an art form as I could. I wanted compression in it, power, eloquence, irony, humor, depth, wisdom. I wanted it to be a great soliloquy in a play ... to be a masterwork, beautifully composed, elegantly said. Now, I probably pulled that off less than I thought. But given these aims – of creating an art form, of drafting a stately soliloquy – I had certain fears.

I was afraid of any questions, any objections, any criticisms, any reaction, except enraptured silence, or uncontained delight at what I was saying and how I was saying it. To listen to questions, or objections, or criticisms, I told myself, will slow the instruction; it'll ruin the delivery; it'll dampen my message; it will disturb my sequence; it'll detain the class; it'll disrupt order. Such arguments can camouflage fear of contradiction, fear of personal inadequacy, fear of being confounded, and perhaps even that deepest perversion in a teacher – fear of lucidity in a learner.

Sad to say, but I was probably thinking like Adolf Hitler during his rise to power. When he finished a spell-binding speech, I assure you, he did not take questions! What an anticlimax that would have been! He marched out while they were still cheering; and he marched out in a clamor of hosannas ... and fear.

"You see these dictators on their pedestals," said Winston Churchill, "surrounded by the bareness of their soldiers and the truncheons of their police. Yet in their hearts there is unspoken, unspeakable fear. They are afraid of words and thoughts, words spoken abroad, thoughts stirring at home, all the more powerful because forbidden. These terrify them. A little mouse, a little tiny mouse of thought appears in the room, and even the mightiest potentates are thrown into panic."[37]

A Course in Miracles has much to say about fear:

"The world as you see it must be in your mind. Do not believe it is outside of yourself, for only by recognizing where it is will you gain control over it. For you do have control over your mind, since the mind is the mechanism of decision."[38]

"Many are at odds with the world they perceive because they think it is antagonistic to them. The problem is not out there; it is inside the perceiver."[39]

"You may be surprised to hear how very different is reality from what you see. You do not realize the magnitude of that one error. It was so vast and so completely incredible that from it a world of total unreality had to emerge."[40]

"A simple question yet remains, and needs an answer. Do you like what you have made? – a world of murder and attack, through which you thread your timid way through constant dangers, alone and frightened, hoping at most that death will wait a little longer before it overtakes you and you disappear. *You made this up.* It is a picture of what you think you are; of how you see yourself."[41]

What you choose to find in the world is "your evaluation of your-self. Choose littleness and you will not have peace, for you will have judged yourself unworthy of it."[42]

"Do you not see that all your misery comes from the strange belief that you are powerless?"[43]

The real you is very important to determine, and it is related to the issue of fear.

My Blessings,

Anselam

Laughing at Fear

Dear Arn,

Now, humor is one of the ways of approaching fear. It is both an evidence of and a stimulant to courage.

Following the British withdrawal in 1940 from Norway, it was proposed that the Royal Marines should have sheaths to protect the exposed muzzles of their rifles from the sharp temperature changes for their next foray into Norway. A pharmaceutical company that specialized in manufacturing condoms was given the job. In due course, the first box was delivered for the Prime Minister's inspection. Winston Churchill looked at the box and muttered, "Won't do." He drew a carton out of the box, shook his head and muttered, "Won't do," again. He opened the carton and took out a packet. "Won't do," he reiterated.

What do you mean it won't do?" an aide asked him. "They are long enough for the muzzles – ten and a half inches."

"It's the labels," said Churchill.

"Labels?"

"Yes," said Churchill. "I want a label for every box, every carton, every packet, saying 'British. Size: Medium.' That will show the Nazis, if they ever recover one of them, who's the master race."[44]

Cheers,

Anselam

Courage

Dear Arn,

Love created courage so that you might never be thwarted by fear. Without courage, love is afraid to be born. Courage is the great facilitator; it makes possible all the virtues, including love. You need it to speak when your colleagues are misguided. You need it to be kind when the world would be cruel. You need it to be yourself when conformity is foolish. You need courage to stand amidst breaking worlds when your concept of self is most endangered. You need courage to trust others, and to love others – because trusting and loving make you vulnerable, and that may make you afraid. It takes courage to be honest, to pursue the truth, even to be reliable under adverse conditions. You even need courage to say that love is the essence of teaching excellence.

Sometimes you can learn courage from the very young. One woman told of a time she worked as a volunteer in Stanford Hospital. "I got to know a little girl named Liza who was suffering from a rare and serious disorder," she said. "Her only chance of recovery appeared to be a blood transfusion from her five-year-old brother, who had miraculously survived the same disease and had developed the antibodies needed to combat the illness. The doctor explained the situation to her little brother and asked the boy if he would be willing to give his blood to his sister." Said the writer, "I saw him hesitate for only a moment before taking a deep breath and saying, 'Yes, I'll do it if it will save Liza.'

"As the transfusion progressed, he lay in a bed next to his sister and smiled, as we all did, seeing the color returning to her cheeks. Then his face grew pale, and his smile faded. He looked up at the doctor and with a trembling voice said, 'Will I start to die right away?'"

The little guy had misunderstood the doctor, and "he thought he was going to have to give [his sister] all his blood."

"Yes, I've learned courage," the woman concluded, "because I've had inspiring teachers."[45]

Blessings,

Anselam

Perfect Love Casts Out Fear

Dear Arn,

Do we ever move beyond courage, you ask.

You may have heard the saying, "Perfect love casts out fear." Now, what does that mean, and is there an example?

In 1945, Gerry Jampolsky went to Stanford University Medical School. There he noted that about a third of all medical students experienced symptoms of the diseases they studied, and some even caught the disease. "I was especially afraid of tuberculosis and was convinced I would eventually contract it and die," he said, "and as it turned out, during my intern year, one of my assignments was to the tuberculosis ward. I had a recurring fantasy that I would take one deep breath in the morning and not breathe for the rest of the day."

On emergency ward one night, Jampolsky encountered a fifty-year-old woman alcoholic with tuberculosis and cirrhosis of the liver. She was vomiting blood and bleeding from her esophagus. Her pulse was faint, her blood pressure fainter, and she was in shock. Giving heart massage, Jampolsky was siphoning the blood from her throat when her respirator failed, and he had to give *mouth to mouth resuscitation*, this to a tubercular! Fortunately, she lived.

When it was over, Jampolsky was absolutely covered in blood. "Suddenly, it occurred to me that not once during that hectic hour had I been afraid," he said. "It was a powerful lesson to realize that when I focused only on helping, I had no fear. The lesson was clear. When a person is concerned only with giving, there is no anxiety. Much later in my life, I was to discover that very often there is also no pain or sense of limitation."[46]

So, Arn, where undiluted love is, fear is not, and where fear is not, courage is unnecessary; or perhaps more accurately, courage has become love. You are infinitely beautiful when you give without a single thought of asking or taking – and you may surprise yourselves as teachers how often you do exactly that. Have you ever noticed that when you intently and whole-heartedly give your gifts of hours and dedication you are quite simply fearless? And quite unconsciously, you have moved beyond the courage to teach, and into love.

Blessings,

Anselam

The Exhilaration of God's Open Sea

Dear Arn,

Alma reminded me the other day of the power of courage. She began with Elbert Hubbard's thought that most people prefer the security of the harbor when what they really need, is the exhilaration of God's open sea. Most do not expand beyond a narrow conception of what they might be. At some point in their lives, they are thrown from the rushing river of life into a side pool, where everything is circumscribed, where often there are friends enough, but where they lose their awareness of the larger picture and where they often group themselves with like-minded souls who see just enough of the outside world to fear it. Cyril Connolly captured what often happened: "Truth is a river that is always splitting up into arms that reunite. Islanded between the arms, the inhabitants argue for a lifetime as to which is the main river."[47]

Love,

Anselam

P.S.

Inside these islands people often create a single, all-dominating way, so rigid that to venture beyond it requires almost super human courage. No wonder Wayne Dyer said the opposite of courage wasn't so much fear, as it was conformity.[48]

Sensitivity

Dear Alma,

What should we do when we see courage? First notice it, then honor it. It is like a tiny bud in a garden, and it may be the first timid attempt at self-expression.

First notice it. Sensitivity is the measure of your emotional and spiritual intelligence. Krishnamurti once said, "Intelligence is not the accumulation of experience and knowledge; but intelligence is the highest form of sensitivity. To be sensitive to everything, to the birds, to the squalor ... to the beauty of a tree ... to the sunset, to the colours, to the reflections, to the movement of a leaf, to the smile of a child, to tears, to laughter, to pain—to be totally sensitive to all that means to be intelligent."[49] So, be sensitive also to courage when you see it.

Lillian was a French Canadian girl from the farming community of River Canard, Ontario. When she was sixteen, her father terminated her schooling so that she might boost the family income. In 1922, during a depression, with English as her second language and few skills, prospects looked dim.

Her father demanded she find a job, but slumping with paltry confidence and low self-esteem, she was downhearted. With scant hope, she rode the bus daily into the "big cities" of Windsor and Detroit, but she was afraid to answer Help Wanted ads, afraid to knock on a door, afraid for her future. In the city she would walk in trepidation, then return home.

"Any luck today, Lill?" her father would ask.

"No, ... no luck today, Dad," she would mumble.

Days passed, the questions became more and more insistent, and Lill knew she would have to act. Finally, she saw a sign at the Carhartt Overall Company in downtown Detroit. "HELP WANTED ... SECRETARIAL. APPLY WITHIN."

Up a long flight of stairs she climbed and tapped lightly on the door where she met Manager Margaret Costello. In poor English, Lill said she was interested in the job . . . and that she was nineteen.

Sensing something amiss, a kindly Margaret guided Lill through the rows of secretaries to a single typewriter at the back of the room. Dispirited, Lill followed.

"Let's see how good you really are," said Margaret, and she asked Lill to type a letter.

It was 11:40 a.m., just before lunch when everyone would be leaving, including herself, Lill thought, *forever*. But for now ... the letter. On first try, she typed a single line of five words, and she made four mistakes. She tossed the paper out and began again. "At noon," she said to herself, "I'll move out with the crowd, and they will never see me again."

On second try, she typed a whole paragraph, but it was still riddled with mistakes. Again, she ditched the paper and started over. This time she finished the letter, still with many errors. It was now five minutes to noon.

Just then Margaret entered. With a hand on Lill's shoulder, she read the letter, then pausing, she said, "Lill, you're doing good work!"

"Lill was stunned," wrote her son and grandson many years later. "She looked at the letter, then up at Margaret. With those simple words of encouragement, her desire to escape vanished, and her confidence was born. Lill thought, 'Well, if she thinks it's good, then it must be.... I think I'll stay.'

"Lill did stay at Carhartt Overall Company, for fifty-one years, through two world wars and a Great Depression, through eleven presidents and six prime ministers" – all because someone with the gift of sensitivity had noticed courage in a shy and uncertain girl, and in a moment of love had nourished it.[50]

Blessings,

Anselam

Faith

Dear Alma,

Faith can also stimulate courage – because faith, strongly held, is a form of assurance, and assurance is a defense against fear. When you are assured, you are not afraid.

There are many stories of faith in the *Chicken Soup for the Soul* series, and here is one.

Cindy Dee Holms is an educator and a health care provider. She works with children infected with AIDS, and they have taught her many things, particularly courage.

She knew young Tyler, a lad born infected with HIV, who contracted the illness from his mother. Medications kept him alive, and at age five he carried a devise in a backpack that pumped medicine through a tube into a vein in his chest. As well, he sometimes needed oxygen.

Tyler took the disease in stride and played anyway, as young boys do. Weighed down with his pump and backpack, he raced round the backyard pulling an oxygen tank in his wagon. His energetic spirit inspired all who saw him, and his mother joked that he was here, there, and everywhere so fast he ought to wear red, so that whenever she looked for him, she could spot him with certainty.

As the disease wore on, Tyler's energy flagged, as did his mother's. She spoke to him of death and told him it would soon overtake her too. Then they would be together again in heaven.

"A few days before his death," said Cindy, "Tyler beckoned me over to his hospital bed and whispered, 'I might die soon. I'm not scared. When I die, please dress me in red. Mom promised she's coming to heaven too. I'll be playing when she gets there, and I want to make sure she can find me.'"51

Love,

Anselam

How Much Freedom?

Dear Alma,

So you are teaching art and wonder how much freedom you should allow.

Helen Buckley once wrote a powerful short story that may help answer your question.

It was the story of a little boy in a big school. One day his teacher said, "Today we will make a picture." And the boy was pleased because he loved making pictures of lions and tigers, and chickens and cows, and trains and boats. Immediately, he took his box of crayons and began to draw.

But his teacher said, "Wait, it is not time to begin." When everyone seemed ready, she told them what they were to draw – flowers. That pleased the lad, and he began to make a bouquet of lovely flowers of all colors and shapes and sizes.

But his teacher said, "Wait, let me show you how." And she made a red flower on a green stem, and told the children to begin.

The little boy did as he was told. He liked his own flowers better, but he did not tell the teacher.

A week or so later, the teacher announced that they were going to make things out of clay. That pleased the boy, and he began to work the clay into the animals of the zoo: the snakes, the elephants, the mice, and then cars and busses.

But his teacher said, "Wait, it is not time to begin." When everyone seemed ready, she told them what they were to make – a dish. That pleased the lad, and he thought of all sorts of dishes, of all shapes and sizes.

But the teacher said, "Wait, let me show you how." And she showed the class how to make a single deep dish. "There, now you may begin," she said.

The little boy did as he was told. He liked his dishes better, but he did not tell the teacher.

So the boy learned to wait and to watch and to follow directions; and he made a deep dish just like the teacher's.

A while later, the boy and his family moved to another city and another school. The first day there his new teacher said, "Let us make a picture." "Good," thought the little boy, and he waited to hear what he should draw. But the teacher didn't say anything. The other students began their work, and the little boy did not know what to do.

"What should we make?" he asked. "I don't know until you make it," said the teacher. "How should I do it?" said the boy. "Any way you want," said the teacher. "Any color?" asked the boy. "Any color," said the teacher. "If everyone made the same picture and used the same colors, how would I know who made what?" "I don't know," said the little boy.

So the little boy made a red flower with a green stem.[52]

Now, Alma, this is a tragic story for the lad and his first teacher. So here is what you might do. Tell the story, then ask yourself how you would end it, what sequel you would add, what additional stanzas you would introduce.

One of my students wrote:

> "I don't know," said the little boy.
>
> And he began to make a red flower with a green stem.
>
> He looked at his flower.
>
> Then he looked at his crayons.
>
> He remembered how he used to see things.

How he used to see life.

He picked up his blue crayon

And then a pink one and a purple one.

Soon he had a lollipop tree next to his red and green flower.

And a rainbow ledge for the background,

A red sun and pink clouds.

He looked at his picture and smiled.

The world looked real again.[53]

Love and freedom are ever companions. This is because love does not dictate or demand, enslave or imprison; it does not control, confine or command; it does not extort, nor does it even have expectations as if it were owed something; it does not insist, nor even suggest, without invitation. Love goes hand in hand with freedom because love respects each soul so much that it won't compel the soul to do anything. Disrespect is invariably attached to command, confinement, and compulsion. Freedom respects, because it supremely honors the choice of the individual.

Perhaps because children are children, the teacher may often have to limit freedom in the interests of class decorum or child safety, but wherever the opportunity arises, always try to offer the greatest degree of freedom with the love you express as a teacher. And the offering will strengthen the love immeasurably.

Love,

Anselam

Being Non-Possessive

Dear Alma,

If I began teaching again tomorrow, I would try to teach the meaning of love – because love is the supreme human experience. Love is amiable, attentive and compassionate, generous, gentle and grateful. It is merciful, patient and kind, tactful, timely, infinitely unfolding and ever-welcoming. It is non-intrusive, non-judgmental and non-possessive. *Non-possessive.*

"I appreciate whatever God gives me, but I don't miss it when it is gone," said Yogananda. "Someone once gave me a beautiful coat and hat, an expensive outfit. Then began my worry. I had to be concerned about not tearing it or soiling it. It made me uncomfortable. I said, 'Lord, why did you give me this bother?' One day I was to lecture in Trinity Hall here in Los Angeles. When I arrived at the hall and started to remove my coat, the Lord told me. 'Take away your belongings from the pockets.' I did so. When I returned to the cloakroom after my lecture, the coat was gone. I was angry, and someone said, 'Never mind, we will get you another coat.' I replied, 'I am not angry because I lost the coat, but because whoever took it didn't take the hat that matches it, too!'"[54]

Love is non-possessive. Remember your students are not *yours*. Some teachers are very possessive of "their" students, but when they are thus, they do not love them.

Blessings,

Anselam

Healing

Dear Alma,

I am so sorry to hear of the traffic deaths of the twin girls from your grade three class. Pray for the protection of their family and their classmates, and pray for them. The helpfulness of prayer does not end when someone passes into spirit. Be a protective spirit yourself. Recognize that you have that ability, which is latent in everyone, and active in all who know who they are.

Anyone who knows who she is, is a natural healer because she is not contorted by anxiety or fear. She sees straight, she knows her strength, and she acknowledges the same strength in her pupils, even if they may not recognize it yet. She feels wholeness in herself, and she honors wholeness in others, even though they may seem impaired in mind and body.

You may think it is an illusion to see health where sickness seems to be, or dignity where self-pity or self-loathing seems to be – but seeing health and dignity in people is a requirement in healing; in fact, it is a requirement in seeing everything aright. You see past their actions, their misgivings, to an inner core of inherent dignity.

Look at very frightened people, and you will see that their awareness of that inherent dignity has departed.

Concerning the matter of death, there is a story Krishnamurti often had his friend and biographer, Pupul Jayakar, repeat. It concerns the nature of time and the illusions in life.

Narada, a musical gossip who consorted with the gods, once met Vishnu, the Preserver, in a grove of trees, and he asked the god the secret of maya, how this world was really illusion.

Vishnu agreed to teach the secret, but wanted Narada to get him a drink of water first. So Narada went into the forest, and he came upon a house and knocked at the door. An inconceivably beautiful young woman answered, smiling at him with her wide, lotus eyes, and immediately he fell in love with her. In a moment, he forgot his purpose, and he stayed for days in her affectionate company. Eventually, almost inevitably, he married her, the years passed in delight, and they had children.

One day, the rains came and did not stop, and the river rose and swept away their home. Frightened, Narada waded out, his wife in one hand, a child in the other and another child on his shoulders. But the flood kept rising to his chest, to his chin, and Narada lost his grip on one child, and then the other, and now, terrified in the darkness and the torrent, he held his wife's hand until he could no longer, and she, too, was swept away. Alone, Narada cried out to the gods in despair.

Suddenly a voice answered: "Ten minutes have passed. Where is my glass of water?"[55]

Helen Schucman, the scribe for *A Course in Miracles*, said something similar. One evening she was brushing her hair when she saw her whole life "symbolized by a golden line stretching infinitely backward and infinitely forward. The time interval representing my present life seemed so incredibly tiny that it could easily have been overlooked entirely unless one looked very carefully for it along the line." She felt that she had seen eternity.[56] Despite appearances, there is a timelessness to all lives, even those that disappear from our view.

Love,

Anselam

Giving Space

Dear Alma,

There is an entry in Krishnamurti's *Journal*, written in April 1975, that relates to your predicament. Let me quote it, then comment.

"Even so early in the morning, the sun was hot and burning. There wasn't a breeze and not a leaf was stirring. In the ancient temple it was cool and pleasant; the bare feet were aware of the solid slabs of rocks, their shapes and their unevenness. Many thousands of people must have walked on them for a thousand years. It was dark there after the glare of the morning sun and in the corridors there seemed to be few people that morning and in the narrow passage it was still darker. This passage led to a wide corridor which led to the inner shrine. There was a strong smell of flowers and the incense of many centuries. And a hundred Brahmans, freshly bathed, in newly washed white loin cloths, were chanting.

Sanskrit is a powerful language, resonant with depth. The ancient walls were vibrating, almost shaking to the sound of a hundred voices. The dignity of the sound was incredible and the sacredness of the moment was beyond the words. It was not the words that awakened this immensity but the depth of the sound of many thousands of years held within these walls and in the immeasurable space beyond them. It was not the meaning of those words, nor the clarity of their pronunciation, nor the dark beauty of the temple but the quality of sound that broke walls and the limitations of the human mind. The song of a bird, the distant flute, the breeze among the leaves, all these break down the walls that human beings have created for themselves.

"In the great cathedrals and lovely mosques, the chants and the intoning of their sacred books—it is the sound that opens the heart, to tears and beauty. Without space there's no beauty; without space you have only walls and measurements; without space there's no depth; without space there's only poverty, inner and outer. You have so little space in your mind; it's so crammed full of words, remembrances, knowledge, experiences and problems. There's hardly any space left, only the everlasting chatter of thought. And so your museums are filled and every shelf with books. Then you fill the places of entertainment, religious or otherwise. Or you build a wall around yourself, a narrow space of mischief and pain. Without space, inner or outer, you become violent and ugly.

"Everything needs space to live, to play and to chant. That which is sacred cannot live without space. You have no space when you hold, when there is sorrow, when you become the centre of the universe. The space that you occupy is the space that thought has built around you and that is misery and confusion. The space that thought measures is the division between you and me, we and they. This division is endless pain. There's that solitary tree in the wide, green, open field."[57]

Sorrow is suffocation, Alma. You spoke of a little girl, nine years old, whose younger twin sisters were killed by a car beside the school grounds. You went to the funeral, and you were with the parents and the girl, comforting. Many months passed, and one day the girl began crying again. Your tender heart poured out for her, and you cried with her, so hard and so long that you could not teach in the next hour, and the little girl herself became hysterical.... Gasping in sorrow, you both could scarcely breathe, for intense sorrow is a form of suffocation. It is an attachment to an airless space containing nothing but grief.

Sympathy carried too far can lead to serious emotional instability. When you comfort, try not to magnify the sadness, feeding it, inflating it. Compulsive sympathy can do that – it can worsen the sense of loss, it can literally bind the distress to the girl, closing the space around her until she can see and feel nothing else....

Krishnamurti was right: "Everything needs space to live, to play, to chant. That which is sacred cannot live without space. You have no space when you hold sorrow."

Devotedly,

Anselam

Breaking Limitations

Dear Alma,

You are correct. There is more in Krishnamurti's story than I suggested. Krishnamurti was interested in breaking the limitations we place on ourselves, and when we do that, we break out into fields around us. You have a new interest – an elementary science club – and Arn is cultivating a new enthusiasm for the theatre. In each case, you have moved beyond a limited self and into the delight of another open space. The more things that fascinate you, the greater your potential to expand beyond your restricted sense of self. Share these things with your students, so that they will cultivate this attitude of delightful expansion.

Can you not see that there is an infinity of space beyond where you presently stand?

Boredom is the human impulse for more, for the life in spaces beyond our present experience.

Love,

Anselam

War

Dear Arn,

Beware of a personality clash that may be developing between you and one of your students.

Always remember Karl Kraus's comment on war:

"War is, at first, the hope that one will be better off; next, the expectation that the other fellow will be worse off; then, the satisfaction that he isn't any better off; and finally the surprise at everyone's being worse off."[58]

So it is with personality clashes too.

If you attack a student, and many teachers have done so, you will, indeed, discover that everyone is worse off – you, the student, and the entire class. War between a teacher and a student is absolutely ruinous to every ideal of a teaching master, let alone his peace of mind.

Do make amends at your first opportunity, and your sleep will return.

Blessings,

Anselam

P.S. Remember, it is exceedingly rare for a student to initiate a reconciliation with a teacher. So *you* must act, before your differences intensify.

Mentoring

Dear Arn,

You are having trouble in your school with what you call a "rene-gade gang of grade tens." In a crowd, they even hiss at incoming teachers.

What to do?

Have you considered a mentoring program that might support these "renegades" and give them a more hopeful spirit? Such a program has many benefits – it could reduce smoking and drug use and absenteeism; it could discourage dropping out; it could build relationships, friendships, a sense of community.

The object of mentoring should be the joining of two minds, not to create dependence, nor to entrench rank, but to cultivate the full flowering of two personalities: the leader and the appren-tice, the helper and the helped. Both grow in the encounter – the helper through the natural blessings in service and the added insights in working with, and learning from, a particular soul; the helped, through the exposure to excellence and the grand potential of becoming a master.

Never forget the great importance of the quality of the mentor-ing relationship. At its best, it is mutually supportive, mutually hopeful and mutually life-affirming. Even if the specific need for a mentor passes away, the general need for such relationships never dies.

Of course, any superb mentor is also a healer. That's what men-toring often is – healing a perceived disability, and the greatest healing is always the revitalization of self-respect. You mention one of the "renegades" as having low self-esteem. Inquire as to the others and their estimate of themselves.

"You will never disserve your relationship—nor anyone—by seeing more in another than they are showing you," Neale Walsch is told in *Conversations with God*. "For there is more there. Much more. It is only their fear that stops them from showing you. If others notice that you see them as more, they will feel safe to show you what you obviously already see."[59] Later, God added, "An overall guideline might be this: When in doubt, always err on the side of compassion. The test of whether you are helping or hurting [is always]—are your fellow humans enlarged or reduced as a result of your help? Have you made them bigger or smaller? More able or less able?"[60]

We are talking about positive, supportive relationships. Joining, sharing, helping – not separating, isolating, ignoring. The medical literature on the benefits of positive, supportive relationships is incontestable.

Cheers,

Anselam

P.S. Perhaps this letter was not necessary after all, given the news you have just conveyed by telephone. Congratulations on resolving the personality clash (mentioned in your last letter), with such tact and understanding, particularly the acknowledgement of your own responsibility in the little tempest. The genuine, forgiving temperament of the student touched you deeply, didn't it? In that moment you each glimpsed the beauty of the other's soul – and that is the purpose of all great teaching. Well done!

The Medicos

Dear Alma and Arn,

So you both have been discussing the value and meaning of supportive leadership. Let me try to show the value of supportive and loving relationships by pointing to legitimate medical studies.

Many studies have shown that people who feel loved and supported have several advantages.

Between 1979 and 1994, eight *massive* community based studies, from California to Finland, examined the link between social isolation, and death and disease from all causes. These were reviewed by Dean Ornish in his important book, *Love and Survival.* "Those who were socially isolated had at least two to five times the risk of premature death from all causes when compared to those who had a strong sense of connection and community," noted Ornish. In Sweden, 17 000 and women aged 29 to 74 were tracked for six years. The isolates and the lonely had four times the risk of dying prematurely in that span. In Holland, researchers interviewed 2800 Dutch citizens aged 55 to 85, and they discovered that those who saw themselves as enveloped by a loving, supportive circle of friends diminished their likelihood of dying by half when compared with isolates who reported feelings of emotional separation.[61]

At the University of Texas Medical School Thomas Oxman and colleagues studied the relationship of social support and spirituality to mortality in men and women six months after elective open-heart surgery. They had two questions:

"Do you participate regularly in organized social groups (clubs, sports, civic activities, church)?

"Do you draw strength and comfort from your religious or spiritual faith (whatever that faith might be)?"

Those who did not regularly participate in social groups were four times more likely to die six months after surgery. Those without strength and comfort from a faith were three times more likely to succumb in six months. And those with neither the social support nor the spiritual support had a sevenfold increased risk of dying six months after surgery![62]

These and many other studies show that loving support and positive relationships are nothing less than life giving and life affirming.

So what can you do in your classrooms and schools to foster *vitality* itself?

With Affection,

Anselam

Fanaticism

Dear Arn,

You have been studying the fanatics of history, and there are many varieties of fanaticism, often stemming from the merciless and unrelenting embrace of some ideal.

The guide Seth once considered the commandment, "Thou shalt not kill," and he suggested a refinement: "Thou shalt not kill even in the pursuit of your ideals."

"What does that mean?" Seth asked. "In practical terms it would mean that you would not wage war for the sake of peace. It would mean that you did not kill animals in experiments, taking their lives in order to protect the sacredness of *human* life...."

"You are a fanatic if you *consider* possible killing for the pursuit of your ideal. For example, your ideal may be—for ideals differ—the production of endless energy for the uses of [humankind], and you may believe so fervently in that idea—this added convenience to life—that you consider the hypothetical possibility of that convenience being achieved at the risk of losing some lives along the way. That is fanaticism.

"'Certainly some lives may be lost along the way, but overall, mankind will benefit.' That is the usual argument. The sacredness of life cannot be sacrificed for life's convenience, or the quality of life itself will suffer. In the same manner, say, the ideal is to protect human life, and in the pursuit of that ideal you give generations of various animals deadly diseases, and sacrifice their lives. Your justification may be that people have souls and animals do not, or that the quality of life is less in the animals, but regardless of those arguments this is fanaticism—and the quality of human life itself suffers as a result, for those who sacrifice any kind of life along the way lose some respect for all life, human life included."[63]

In truth,

Anselam

Egocentrism

Dear Arn,

I was always on the lookout for memorable stories to illustrate a point. It was a weakness, perhaps, but I could never fully understand an abstract principle without an example. Once I had the example, the principle lived, and its beauty appeared like a rainbow.

While you are discussing fanatics and trying to teach connectedness with everything, instead of separation, a sense of being part of the whole rather than an egocentric speck in an alien universe, you might remember Baba's illustration:

"The physical universe contains billions of suns, each with its own world; there are countless planets, big and small and innumerable beings, and in this entire vast universe, the earth is smaller than even a tiny drop; on this earth, India is just a little country. In this little country there is a small state. In this small state is a very little district. In this little district, there is just a minor village. In this village there is an insignificant little house. And in this little house there sits a very small body....Isn't it ludicrous to think that such a small body could ever feel egoistic and blown up with self-importance considering its minute size in this huge universe?"[64]

Blessings,

Anselam

Crows

Dear Arn,

Yes, there are other stories Baba has told that make a point with the same memorable clarity.

One day Baba was talking about a bird that no one seems to like much – the crow. But the crow had a sense of unity, he said. "When it discovers a morsel of food it never eats alone. It caws repeatedly until its kith and kin gather at that place."[65]

The story is about the great importance of sharing one's joys.

Blessings,

Anselam

Oneness

Dear Alma,

Yes, this theme of oneness is very important for youngsters to grasp and to embrace.

How can you help them?

A story from *When Elephants Weep* might assist.

"One evening in the 1930s, Ma Shwe, a work elephant, and her three-month-old calf were trapped in rising floodwaters in the Upper Taungdwin River in Burma. Elephant handlers rushed to the river when they heard the calf screaming but could do nothing to help, for the steep banks were twelve to fifteen feet high. Ma Shwe held the baby against her body; whenever it began to drift away, she used her trunk to pull the calf back against the current. [But] the fast-rising river soon washed the calf away, and Ma Shwe plunged downstream for fifty yards and retrieved it. She pinned her calf against the bank with her head, then lifted it in her trunk, reared up on her hind legs, and placed it on a rocky ledge five feet above the water. Ma Shwe then fell back into the torrent and disappeared downstream.

"The elephant handlers [watched] the calf, which could barely fit on the narrow ledge where it stood shivering, eight feet below. Half an hour later, J. H. Williams, the British manager of the elephant camp, was peering down at the calf wondering how to rescue her when he heard 'the grandest sounds of a mother's love I can remember. Ma Shwe had crossed the river and was making her way back as fast as she could, calling the whole time—a defiant roar, but to her calf it was music. The two little ears, like little maps of India, were cocked forward listening to the only sounds that mattered, the call of her mother.' When

Ma Shwe saw her calf, safe on the other side of the river, her call changed to the rumble that elephants typically make when pleased. The two elephants were left where they were. By morning Ma Shwe had crossed the river, no longer in flood, and the calf was off the ledge."[66]

Love,

Anselam

When the Earth Touched the Moon

Dear Alma,

I have thought more about how you might teach oneness. Most ecological and environmental programs, of course, help, but you might have your grade threes go out after a rainstorm, when they will see many earthworms stranded on pavement, on carports, sidewalks, tennis courts. If the worms cannot grope their way to porous earth, they will all die in the hot, drying sun, just as people die of thirst in the desert. Or they will be crushed under heel or run over.

You can teach respect for even this seemingly lowest form of life, by finding a safe place, taking a pencil and gently steering it under the lost worm, then placing the worm on grass or soil where it can reenter its home, the earth.

Or tell a story that appeals to children's emotions, especially their innate compassion. Generally, if the story touches you, it will touch them. Keep it simple and uncomplicated.

Here is a story I once wrote that you may use if you wish. It is called "When the Earth Touched the Moon," and it is about the universal feeling of being lost, separated, isolated, alone. It is about the connections in our life and our world that remind us how we are related, how we touch each other, even when we are as far apart as the earth from the moon....

It was Hanson's first visit to the mountains, and the day started out fine, but he did wonder a bit about the camp leaders. The hikers were tramping through the forest when one of the leaders told Hanson to go the other way around a clump of trees, and they would meet on the other side. Sure enough, when Hanson got to the other side, the leader wasn't there.

So Hanson kept walking. But no matter how far he went, or how many trees he looked around, no one was there. "I'm half lost," he mumbled to himself. But he was wrong – he was completely lost.

It was sundown when he rested at a lake. No one was there, and he seemed so alone. It was so silent and so still, and he listened for the faintest whisper.

Before long, the moon came out. But that didn't help the rescuers who were still searching for Hanson miles away, near that first clump of trees he had walked around.

As Hanson huddled beside a big evergreen, he gathered pine cones around him to keep warm, and he soon fell asleep.

And he dreamed a strange dream.

In it he asked the spirit of the earth-"Have you ever been lost?"

"Yes," said the earth. "I have looked into the endless space of the skies and felt very alone."

"I know what you mean," said Hanson, gazing at the distant stars.

Then Hanson turned to the lake, glowing in the moonlight, and asked, "Have you ever been lost?"

"Yes," said the lake, "I have looked in all directions and never seen another one like me. I think I'm the only lake here."

"I know what you mean," said Hanson, peering down the dark valley.

And that thought brought another one just like it, only worse.

A real person now appeared in Hanson's dream. It was a little baby girl, left alone in a garbage dump.

"Is there no one to care for you?" asked Hanson.

"No," said the spirit of the little girl. "I was unwanted."

"Then you are lost too," said Hanson, very concerned.

"Yes," said the little girl who seemed to be waiting ever so calmly to die.

Shaking his head, Hanson tried to change his dream, and he thought perhaps a different question would change it. Now, this question was barely different, but sometimes just barely is just enough.

He called back to the spirit of the earth: "Are you still lost?"

"Oh, no," said the earth. "A strange thing happened one night. It was one of those things that occurs only once in a long while – an eclipse. I looked into the sky and saw my own shadow touching the moon. So, I called out to the moon, who for years I thought was dead, and I said I was sorry for causing darkness to fall on him.

"The moon surprised me. So delighted was he that I had finally spoken to him that he immediately forgot he couldn't see properly, and he told me that he had watched me forever, and that he was my younger brother. All this time he thought I was the one who was dead because I had never spoken to him."

"After that," said the earth, "I never felt lost again."

Then Hanson asked the spirit of the lake, "Are you still lost?"

"Oh, no," the lake said. "A strange thing happened one day – I actually looked at myself for the first time. I had often thought of myself, but never really looked at myself. In the north I saw a stream pouring into me, and I was sure I would burst, but just before I did, I saw the stream emptying out in the south.

"The stream told me he had been part of me all along, the best part, the talking part. And he told the ocean he was the life of the lake, and the lake surely did need life, because it hadn't said a word in ten centuries!"

"It wasn't all my fault," chuckled the lake, "as it is hard to hear a trickle talk!"

"But once we smiled together and laughed together, I never felt lost again."

Then Hanson hurried to the little girl, the one he was most worried about because she was so weak and tiny.

"Are you still lost?" he asked, anxiously.

"Oh no," said the little girl. "A strange thing happened the day after you saw me. I was about to give up, when a kind woman came. She held me and fed me, and wanted me and loved me."

"What about you, Hanson, are you still lost?"

Before he could say no, he awoke to shouts of his name.

It was early morning, and his parents and grandparents were the first to see him lying on the earth beside the lake, beneath the moon still watching from the skies. As his rescuers hugged him, he told of his dream.

"The earth was not lost when it saw itself touching the moon," Hanson began warmly. "And the lake and the baby were not lost when...."

And so, Alma, with such a story, or one you might make up yourself, you can remind your pupils that there is a beautiful sense of being "found" when we recognize our loving relationship with all things and people. To feel love is never to be lost again.

"For in the end we will conserve only what we love," said Baba Dioum, "we will love only what we understand, and we will understand only what we have been taught."[67]

Love,

Anselam

Judgment

Dear Alma,

You have a student, named Mary, now in grade 11, who was told by a teacher some years ago that she would never amount to anything, that she lacked ability. And the student, wavering from anger to dejection all these years, has never forgotten this judgment.

What to do?

Let me quote something from *A Course in Miracles* that long ago I memorized. It is a passage not often fully grasped by readers.

"The aim of our curriculum, unlike the goal of the world's learning, is the recognition that judgment in the usual sense is impossible. This is not an opinion, but a fact. In order to judge anything rightly, one would have to be fully aware of an inconceivably wide range of things; past, present and to come. One would have to recognize in advance all the effects of his judgments on everyone and everything involved in them in any way. And one would have to be certain there is no distortion in his perception, so that his judgment would be wholly fair to everyone on whom it rests now, and in the future. Who is in a position to do this? Who except in grandiose fantasies would claim this for himself?"[68]

So the teacher, perhaps in a fit of frustration, told Mary she was nothing and would amount to the same. Perhaps Mary now can see that the teacher could not possibly have had the infinite understanding that would have allowed him to make the judgment. He would have to have known Mary's entire past, the gifts she was born with, the nurturing her parents afforded, the fact that she had an aunt who brought out in her a host of talents in needle point, crocheting, embroidery, quilting, petit point; the fact that she was an exceptional swimmer, that even when she was seven, she had a way with younger children. The teacher would have to have known many, many things about her at the very moment he condemned her: things he did not know, things he was not aware of – the fact that Mary, then twelve, had no mother, but was expected to be a mother herself to her younger sister, and that the sister was vomiting all night, with her young surrogate mother by her side. The teacher would have to have known the light of compassion in that twelve-year-old girl that night.

And the teacher would have to have known the incomprehensible richness of that light, how it touches the younger sibling still, and just as importantly, what that light is destined to be, who it will comfort in the future.

Only a person of very great wisdom and specific knowledge could know those things, and anyone who did know them (and I assure you that there are some who do know), not one of them would ever cast a cruel judgment.

Now, the second part of the admonition is that "One would have to recognize in advance all the effects of his judgments on everyone and everything involved in them in any way." So the teacher who judged would have to have known the effect of his judgment.

When someone tells you that you will never amount to anything, what effect does it have on you? A very wide spectrum of effect is possible. You could accept his judgment as final and live the rest of your life in fulfillment of it, or you could accept some part of it, perhaps as it pertains to some things you think you don't do well anyway, or you could reject the entire condemnation and demonstrate later the utter falsity of it.

Now, how in the world does the teacher know what you will do? How could he ever know the millions of choices you will make related to success or failure over the next half century and more? A teacher who will condemn you is utterly incapable of knowing all these things.

What we humanly know is less than a billionth part of what we do not know, and yet that speck which cannot support anything is the basis of our judgments about everything.

The third part of the admonition is, "One would have to be certain there is no distortion in his perception, so that his judgment would be wholly fair to everyone on whom it rests now, and in the future." Now, when the teacher judged Mary, he also judged the father and the aunt and the sister and everyone else crucially involved in the life of the girl. The teacher proclaimed, in effect, that nothing all these helpers and teachers might do in serving the student could ever assist her in becoming something, in succeeding. The judgment was clearly unfair to all these people, each one of whom would play an important role in affirming Mary's worth. The father's dedication to his family, bereft of his love mate, would kindle a fire in the heart of his young daughter, a fire of devotion to the lost, the hurt, the uncertain. And wherever that conflagration burns, I assure you, you have amounted to something.

The younger sister has never forgotten Mary's eternal outpouring of kindness. In time, the purity of her gratitude will dawn on Mary, and in that moment, Mary will know instinctively that gratitude is the only lens through which we can see love because it is the surest sign that love has been recognized. She will know that gratitude is love's natural reaction to love. And she will teach these things to her own children. And anyone who has learned them, I assure you, will have amounted to something.

The teacher's judgment was distorted by ignorance, by lack of clear seeing or clairvoyance. Nor was it fair to you, a person this teacher did not even know when he rejected Mary. How could he have divined that you, of all people, would come into Mary's life? You, who would teach her the beauty of what she is.

When you judge anyone you also judge the Creator who made her and who is a priceless part of her.

Love,

Anselam

Supportive Leadership

Dear Alma,

What is the most important single factor in your leadership, you ask.

That it be supportive; that it generate relationships that are supportive.

If I were beginning my teaching career over again, I would watch for things that are inherently unsupportive or disconnected – things I often missed when I was teaching. I would watch for separation and isolation, the alienated and the forsaken, the ignored, the oppressed, the outsiders, the orphans. I would watch for those indifferent to nature and their surroundings; for those without kinship ties to other life forms; for souls without a sense of place or belonging; for the friendless, the abandoned, the beset and the distraught. And with all these separated souls, I would not agree with their sad estimate of themselves, for that would consummate the separation. I would go out of my way to show respect for those ignored by others. In a word, I would be more supportive.

"Have constructive thoughts, consoling words, compassionate acts," says Sai Baba in a touching refrain. "Be on the look-out for eyes filled with tears, hearts heaving in sighs.

"Shower cheer on the sad; soothe those who have lost the way; close your eyes to the faults of others, but keep them open to discover your own. Even in persons of unpleasant nature, be aware that God is in the heart of that person. Have that aspect in mind and treat that person from that viewpoint to the best of your ability. In time that person will respond, and his nature will change."[69]

At one point, Christ, in *The URANTIA Book*, says that he will stop at nothing to restore respect to those who have lost it.[70] And neither now would I.

Love,

Anselam

An Uncommon Virtue

Dear Alma,

The Mother who taught with the sage Aurobindo told this story.

High in the clouds, hidden from most mortals, was a splendid palace, the Palace of Truth, where a festival was held one day for the gods and goddesses who represent the Virtues.

In the vestibule of the Palace was the Hall of Intelligence where the light near the floor was a soft sapphire hue, becoming clearer toward the diamond chandeliers above. "The Virtues came separately," said the Mother, "but soon formed congenial groups, full of joy to find themselves for once, at least, together, for they are usually so widely scattered throughout the world and the worlds, isolated amid so many alien beings."

Sincerity was Mistress of Ceremonies, and next to her stood Humility and Courage, the latter holding the hand of a woman veiled, but with searching, discerning eyes. Her name was Prudence.

Around them passed Charity and her twin sister, and inseparable companion, Justice. And with them were Gentleness, Patience, Kindness, Compassion and others. All had arrived, or so they thought.

Just then, at the golden gate, a newcomer appeared. Reluctantly, the guards allowed her entry, for they knew her not, and she looked so young and slight, her white dress so simple, almost poor. Ill at ease in the brilliance, she wondered where to turn.

Sensing her embarrassment and consulting briefly with others, Prudence went to her. "We who are gathered here, and who all know each other by our names and our merits, are surprised at your coming, for you appear to be a stranger to us, or at least we do not seem to have ever seen you before," said Prudence. "Would you be so kind as to tell us who you are?"

The newcomer answered with a sigh:

"Alas! I am not surprised that I appear to be a stranger in this palace, for I am so rarely invited anywhere.

"My name is Gratitude."[71]

Love,

Anselam

Another Virtue

Dear Arn,

You are laughing at the funny things that happen in school, and laughing in a positive way. Humor is indispensable for teachers, and it is one of the common elements found among outstanding mentors. Every teacher experiences a degree of distress, and every time of distress, especially if prolonged, requires a psychological stabilizer, like a mind-gyro, to maintain the emotional equilibrium of the strained and suffering.

Humor is a priceless balancer. It is the divine antidote for the exaltation of the ego, *and* for the destitution of the self. It is attracted to the poles of human experience – from delusions of grandeur to delusions of insignificance. And it has the power to dissolve either. Those who can laugh at themselves are armor-plated, protected from the folly of taking themselves too seriously.

Humor unerringly seeks out the extremist who insists overmuch on his own way, who stifles opposition and denies human choice, who is so filled with a cause that there is no room in him for common sense.

One time, my brother was experiencing difficulty with his son, then fourteen. My brother celebrated his birthday (ironically the two had the same birthday), and his son gave him this card: "Dear dad, despite all the turmoil ... the conflicts ... the screaming and the tantrums ... you're doing just fine."

Once when I was teaching *The Iliad*, the students were reading in silence, and one of them was asleep at his desk, his face flat on the book I loved. "A little hard on the eyes, isn't it, Jim?" I said.

Without moving, he muttered, "I know – that's why I got 'em closed!"

Of course, a spontaneous, innate sense of humor serves best. But you, who teach language arts, journalism and social studies, might also watch for humorous quotations to spice your fare. Here are some I have found:

During the first Gulf War there was an Iraqi radio announcer called "Baghdad Betty." One day Betty announced to the Allied, mostly American troops: "While you are away, movie stars are taking your women. Robert Redford is dating your girlfriend, Tom Selleck is kissing your lady, Bart Simpson is making love to your wife."

Senator William Scott of Virginia was listening to a Pentagon briefing in which army officials began telling him about   missile *silos*. "Wait a minute," he interrupted. "I'm not interested in agriculture. I want the military stuff."

An inscription on the grave of a British soldier in northwestern modern day Pakistan reads:"Here lies Captain Ernest Bloomfield, Accidentally shot by his orderly March 2nd 1879. Well done, good and faithful servant."

From our athletes:

"My sister's expecting a baby," said North Carolina basketballer Chuck Nevitt, "and I don't know if I am going to be an uncle or an aunt."

"I've never had major knee surgery on any other part of my body," said Winston Bennett, University of Kentucky basketballer.

Remarked George Rogers, New Orleans running back, "I want to gain 1500 or 2000 yards, whichever comes first."

From our politicians:

"That lowdown scoundrel deserves to be kicked to death by a jackass-and I'm just the one to do it." A congressional candidate, Texas.

"Why can't the Jews and Arabs just sit down together and settle this like good Christians?" Attributed to British Prime Minister Arthur Balfour.

"Outside of the killings, Washington has one of the lowest crime rates in the country." Mayor Marion Barry, Washington, D.C.

"The only way to stop this suicide wave is to make it a capital offense, punishable by death." Irish legislator.

Here is a sign posted by Japanese citizens who heard that General MacArthur was running for the US presidency: "We pray for MacArthur's erection."

Those who disdain foreign languages, might agree with this comment by a US congressman: "If English was good enough for Jesus Christ, it's good enough for me."[72]

Cheers,

Anselam

Hiding Your Brilliance Under a Bushel

Dear Alma and Arn,

Krishnamurti once said, "You know, it is good to hide your brilliance under a bushel, to be anonymous, to love what you are doing and not to show off. It is good to be kind without a name. That does not make you famous, it does not cause your photograph to appear in the newspapers. Politicians do not come to your door. You are just a creative human being living anonymously, and in that there is richness and great beauty."[73]

You may sometimes seem unsure, alone and beset, but your real self always knows its name, its connectedness, its peace. It knows its purpose, its timelessness. It is what it does, and it does what it is, ceaselessly, tirelessly, faithfully, joyfully. It knows it is a light, and it knows that no wind can blow it out. And whenever it helps others, it burns at its brightest, because it is part of the inextinguishable Divine Light.

With affection,

Anselam

Master Teachers

Dear Alma and Arn,

Alma, I am delighted that you have started reading *A Course in Miracles*, and sorry that you are finding parts of it hard going. You ask how it can help you to be a better teacher, and Arn, in listening to Alma, you want the summary of it.

A Course in Miracles says, "a teacher of God [that is, a Master teacher] is anyone who chooses to be one. His qualifications consist solely in this; somehow, somewhere he has made a deliberate choice in which he did not see his interests as apart from someone else's. Once he has done that, his road is established and his direction is sure. A light has entered the darkness. It may be a single light, but that is enough."[74]

This light is the radiance of a different viewpoint. I saw it in Jim Byrne, the master mathematician, as he came down the hall. He didn't care if other teachers dressed in a thrift shop – he wore a suit. Self-assurance, self-respect, good will and absolute mastery of his discipline emanated from him. You could feel it.

I saw this radiance in Al Martin, another superb math teacher who coached our volleyball team as a sidelight. The year my youngest son played for him, we reached the finals. We won game one, lost game two, then the crucial third began. Martin played everyone, and I still see him encouraging and comforting one of the poorer players who had just come off the floor after playing his best. Not even the fury of the game, now reaching a crescendo, interfered with that beautiful communion of gratitude. We won the game in a thrilling finish. Yet my dominant memory is of those two – a young, unsure boy in grade eight, and an old master, three years from retirement, smiling and patting the lad on the back – those two, whose interests had become one.

After winding through 1100 pages, the *Course in Miracles* finally lists ten characteristics of God's master teachers. The first is trust, and all others rest upon it. The second is honesty, and "only the trusting can afford honesty," it says, "for only they can see its value."[75] With no one to trust, we could ill-afford to be honest, because others would surely exploit our openness. And if we could not be honest, we could not be trusted – different circumstances would spur different responses, depending on the degree of threat they evoked. Before long, we would appear very deceptive and very inconsistent. The *Course* says that the term honesty "actually means consistency. There is nothing you say that contradicts what you think or do; no thought opposes any other thought; no act belies your word; and no word lacks agreement with another. Such are the truly honest. At no level are they in conflict with themselves."[76]

A third characteristic is gentleness. Says the speaker, every master teacher "must learn—and fairly early in his training—that harmfulness completely obliterates his function from his awareness. It will make him confused, fearful, angry and suspicious."[77] And in that state you cannot hear anything, especially your inner voice. That voice, remember, "does not command, because it is incapable of arrogance. It does not demand, because it does not seek control. It does not overcome, because it does not attack. It merely reminds."[78] It will not interrupt your conscious mind, nor will it speak above a whisper, and it may also have to contend with a belief system that asserts that the Voice itself does not even exist.

All the attributes of outstanding teachers, says the *Course*, are combined in the word "faithfulness" – a faith in themselves, in their students, in their own positive outlook, in their ability to solve their problems. "True faithfulness," it says, "does not deviate. Being consistent it is wholly honest. Being un-swerving, it is full of trust. Being based on fearlessness, it is gentle. Being certain, it is joyous. And being confident, it is tolerant."[79]

A favorite mentor of mine was Cary F. Goulson. As a student, I knew him at the University of Victoria, British Columbia, where he graced the halls of the education faculty in the mid-1960s and for a generation after. One autumn, many years ago, Goulson attended an unusual reunion.

It was the thirty-seventh anniversary of a grade nine class he had taught. The students had been fourteen or fifteen then and were now over fifty. Back then, Goulson had asked them to write an essay on what they wished to do with their lives, and what kind of person they wanted to be. Now, half a lifetime later, he called the roll and announced he had an assignment to return.

The class fell silent as each received and re-read what he or she had written so long ago. Many thoughts must have raced through their minds – what kind of person would cherish their scribbles for so long? How does a fifty-year-old greet the teenager he or she once was? What, again, does a fourteen-year-old want? What, really, did that teacher seek?

Perhaps some sensed only now what ideals mean to a mentor and a student. Perhaps a few compared their fond hopes to their subsequent comportment. Whatever the musings, some thoughts were self-reflective and self-enquiring. And that elder teacher, *my* teacher, without a trace of judgment, was encouraging those thoughts and those students still. *That*, my friends – *that*, is faithfulness.

With Affection,

Anselam

Stifling Plans

Dear Alma,

You are exhausted from lesson planning and you wonder if there will ever be a time when these "infernal plans" can be set aside.

The answer is yes, but you will have to decide when.

Let me share with you a line from *The URANTIA Book* about Jesus that may seem strange at first:

"Most of the really important things which Jesus said or did seemed to happen casually, 'as he passed by.' There was so little of the professional, the well-planned, or the premeditated in the Master's earthly ministry."[80]

Why?

Because pre-planning everything can straightjacket everything, close the mind to everything *but* the plan. The Master was never defensive in this way, never dismissive of the individual who might ask him whatever he wanted to ask. There weren't some things the Master could handle, and others he was afraid of, which he could conveniently dump from the plan. You know, "We're not going to talk about this, because I'm weak here, so it is not in the plan, and if you bring it up, you'll be out of order." To be completely open, completely respectful, completely loving, he had to honor the spontaneity of the moment, and the great possibility that the discussion would turn in a hundred different directions, and that the help he offered could do likewise.

He did not have to be at a lectern, or in front of a class, or on a soap box, or in some formal setting to be a light, and neither do you. He could be in transit and glow, and so can you. He could minister "as he passed by," and so might you. He was a charming listener, and so are you.

You do not need a detailed plan to be these things. You need only a beautiful vision of yourself.

Bound by their plans, teachers ask too many of the questions in a classroom.

Love,

Anselam

Love

Dear Alma and Arn,

If you develop love, you don't need to develop anything else.

What is there, that a teacher does, that cannot be related to love? If you are loving, you will treat students and colleagues with respect. If you are loving, you will settle for nothing but absolute fairness in assessment, tempered always by kindness. If you are loving, you will be crystal clear in your expectations. You will embrace your subject matter enthusiastically, constantly expanding your mastery of it. You will return assignments promptly, provide feedback systematically and thoughtfully. You will help whenever you hear a call for help. You will welcome student criticism. You won't limit your time for your students or colleagues. You won't seal yourselves off at home, forbidding all contact there. You won't separate your life into moments you can help, and moments you can't. You won't withdraw your gifts of time and energy when you don't see immediate results. You won't hold grudges for perceived slights.

The entire teaching experience can be characterized as an exercise in love. And when something is wrong, applying love to the problem will invariably solve it (or dissolve it as a problem). A teacher who has trouble because she does not provide written requirements or clear verbal requirements, can solve the problem by being more considerate. A teacher who dislikes herself, her own subject matter, the room she is in, the assignments she gives, or the penalties she devises, is encountering a problem of affection. Why solve incoherence in a teacher? Because it is considerate to do so. Why remedy inaudibility? Because it is caring to do so. Why ask for student evaluations? Because it respects them, and you. Ask always, "What would a considerate person do?" and your difficulties will recede. If an assessment procedure is unfair, or a punishment unjust, both are unloving.

A curriculum that devalues the historical and geographical setting in which it exists, or that degrades universalism in favor of patriotism, or that disregards the beauty of a single human soul, is short of one thing – love.

With warmth,

Anselam

Gratitude

I am most grateful to Colleen Kawalilak, Nancy Dudley, Jim Paul, Angela Rokne, Lynn Bosetti, and Kent Donlevy, for their helpful comments on an earlier draft of the *Meditations of Anselam.*

I also thank my dear friends, Larry Wayne and Grace Johnston, for sharing their wisdom.

Endnotes

1 Elbert Hubbard quoted in David C. Jones, ed., *Sayings for Teachers* (Calgary: Detselig, 1997), p. 8.

2 Jack Kornfield, *A Path with Heart* (New York: Bantam, 1993), p. 334.

3 J. Donald Walters quoted in David C. Jones, ed., *Sayings for Leaders* (Calgary: Detselig, 2003), p. 94.

4 Helen MacInnes quoted in Jones, *Sayings for Leaders*, p. 23.

5 John S. Hilsop, *Conversations with Bhagavan Sri Sathya Sai Baba* (Prasanthi Nilayam, India: Sri Sathya Sai Books and Publications nd), pp. 22-23, my italics.

6 Proverb quoted in David C. Jones, ed., *Sayings on Love* (Calgary: Detselig, 2000), p. 71.

7 *A Course in Miracles*, Manual for Teachers, (New York: Viking, 1996), p. 20.

8 Neale Donald Walsch, *Conversations with God*, Book 1 (New York: G.P. Putnam's Sons, 1996), pp. 121, 124, italics in the original.

9 J. Donald Walters, *Little Secrets of Success* (Nevada City: Crystal Clarity Publishers, 1994), day 21.

10 *A Course in Miracles*, Manual for Teachers, p. 1.

11 Yogananda quoted in Jones, *Sayings on Love,* p. 78.

12 Proverb quoted in David C. Jones, ed., *Sayings for Sufferers* (Calgary: Detselig, 1998), p. 10.

13 *The URANTIA Book* (Chicago: URANTIA Foundation, 1981), p. 1732.

14 *A Course in Miracles*, Text, p. 76.

15 Herbert Benson, with Marg Stark, *Timeless Healing: The Power and Biology of Belief* (New York: Scribner, 1996), p. 40.

16 Benson, *Timeless Healing*, p. 32.

17 David C. Jones, ed., *Sayings for Cynics* (Calgary: Detselig, 1999), pp. 23, 25, 38, 47.

18 Ibid., p. 42.

[19] Ibid., p. 71.

[20] My thanks to Gordon Hunter for this joke.

[21] Jones, *Sayings for Cynics*, p. 9.

[22] Ibid., p. 10.

[23] Ibid.

[24] *The URANTIA Book*, p. 557.

[25] Elbert Hubbard, *The Notebook of Elbert Hubbard* (New York: Wise, 1927), p. 89.

[26] Elbert Hubbard 11, *The Philosophy of Elbert Hubbard* (New York: Wise, 1930), p. 92.

[27] George Eliot quoted in Jones, *Sayings for Sufferers*, p. 24.

[28] Erich Fromm quoted in Jones, *Sayings for Suffers*, p. 30.

[29] *A Course in Miracles*, Teachers, p.63.

[30] *The URANTIA Book*, p. 1874.

[31] J. Donald Walters quoted in Jones, *Sayings for Teachers*, p. 42.

[32] Wayne W. Dyer, *The Power of Intention* (Carlsbad Ca., Hay House, 2004), p. 143.

[33] Sai Baba quoted in David C. Jones, ed., *Sayings for Teachers*, p. 22.

[34] *The URANTIA Book*, p. 193.

[35] Silver Birch quoted in Jones, ed., *Saying for Sufferers*, p. 32.

[36] Rama quoted in Jones, *Sayings for Leaders*, p. 65.

[37] Edward R. Murrow and Fred W. Friendly, eds., "I Can Hear It Now: Winston Churchill," Columbia LP KL 5066.

[38] *A Course in Miracles*, Text, pp. 222-223.

[39] Ibid., pp. 222.

[40] Ibid., p. 373.

[41] Ibid., p. 429., italics in the original.

[42] Ibid., p. 306.

[43] Ibid., p. 461.

[44] Dominique Enright, ed., *The Wicked Wit of Winston Churchill* (London: Michael O'Mara Books, 2001), p. 121.

[45] Dan Millman, "On Courage," in Jack Canfield and Mark Victor Hansen, *Chicken Soup for the Soul* (Deerfield Beach, Fla.: Health Communications, 1993), pp. 27-28.

[46] Gerald G. Jampolsky, *Teach Only Love-The Seven Principles of Attitudinal Healing* (Toronto: Bantam, 1983), pp. 5-6.

[47] Cyril Connolly quoted in Jones, *Sayings for Leaders*, p. 82.

[48] Wayne W. Dyer, *Staying on the Path* (Carson, Ca., Hay House, 1995), p. 102.

[49] Susunaga Weeraperuma, *Sayings of J. Krishnamurti* (Delhi: Motilal Banarsidass, 2000), p. 93.

[50] Dedicated to Lillian Kennedy by James M. Kennedy (son) and James C. Kennedy (grandson), "A Lady Named Lill," in Jack Canfield, et.al., *Chicken Soup for the Soul at Work* (Deerfield Beach, Fl.: Health Communications, 1996), pp. 75-77.

[51] Cindy Dee Holms, "Please Dress Me in Red," in Jack Canfield and Mark Victor Hansen, eds., *A 3rd Serving of Chicken Soup for the Soul* (Deerfield Beach, Fl.: Health Communications, 1996), pp. 176-177.

[52] Irene Russell Naested, *Art in the Classroom: An Integrated Approach to Teaching Art in Canadian Elementary and Middle Schools* (Toronto: Harcourt Brace, 1998), pp. 35-37.

[53] Thanks to Kathy Dawson.

[54] Yogananda quoted in Jones, *Sayings on Love*, p. 41.

[55] Pupul Jayakar, *Krishnamurti: A Biography* (San Francisco, Harper and Row, 1986), pp. 294-95.

[56] Kenneth Wapnick, *Absence from Felicity* (Rosecoe, NY: Foundation for "A Course in Miracles," 1991), pp. 129-130.

[57] J. Krishnamurti, *Krishnamurti's Journal* (San Francisco: Harper and Row, 1982), pp. 79-80.

[58] Karl Kraus quoted in Jones, *Sayings for Sufferers*, p. 23.

[59] Neale Donald Walsh, *Conversations with God* 1, p. 141.

[60] Ibid.

[61] Dean Ornish, *Love and Survival* (New York: HarperCollins, 1998), pp. 41-48.

[62] Ibid., pp. 50-51

63 Jane Roberts, *The Individual and the Nature of Mass Events* (New York: Prentice Hall, 1987), pp. 214-215.

64 Tumuluru Krishna Murty, ed., *Digest Collection of Sri Sathya Said Baba's Sayings* (T. Gowri: Tumuluru & Co., Computer Services, 1994), p. 40.

65 Ibid., p.76.

66 Jeffrey Moussaieff Masson and Susan McCarthy, *When Elephants Weep: The Emotional Lives of Animals* (New York: Bantam Doubleday, Dell, 1995), pp. 64-65.

67 Baha Dioum quoted in Jones, *Sayings for Leaders*, p. 13.

68 *A Course in Miracles*, Teachers, p. 26.

69 Sai Baba quoted in Jones, *Sayings for Cynics*, p. 76.

70 *The URANTIA Book*, p.1765.

71 The Mother, *Collected Works of the Mother-Centenary Edition, vol 2. Words of Long Ago* (Pondicherry, India; Sri Aurobindo Ashram Press, 1978), pp. 5-6.

72 Ross and Kathryn Petras, *The 365 Stupidest Things Ever Said*, 1995 Calendar, (New York: Workman Publishing, 1994), January 18, 31; March 2, 22, 26; July 5, October 1, November 1, December 4, 11, 19.

73 Krishnamurti quoted in David C. Jones, ed., *Sayings for Mentors and Tutors* (Calgary: Detselig, 2001), p. 21.

74 *A Course in Miracles*, Teachers, p. 3.

75 Ibid., p. 11.

76 Ibid., p. 10.

77 Ibid., p. 11.

78 *A Course in Miracles*, Text, p. 76.

79 *A Course in Miracles*, Teachers, p. 15.

80 *The URANTIA Book*, p. 1875.